Welcome!
Make Yourself at Home

Welcome! Make Yourself at Home

A New Understanding of Hospitality

VINCENT M. BILOTTA, PH.D.

Copyright © 2022 by Vincent M. Bilotta

All rights reserved, including the right of reproduction in whole or in part, in any form, only with expressed permission in writing from the author and the publisher.

Text designed and composed at Hobblebush Design (www.hobblebush.com)

Printed in the United States of America

ISBN: 978-0-578-38699-7
Library of Congress Control Number: 2022906383

Cover illustration by Julie Vaughn Gearan

Dedicated with love to Denise (Gearan) Bilotta, my wife, life partner, and a Clinical Social Worker, whose gracious presence as a natural welcomer started our personal journey of hospitality when, as a newlywed, she initiated a tradition of inviting groups of four people to our small apartment in Pittsburgh for hot chocolate and homemade sugar cookies. During our 54 years together, we have welcomed and invited hundreds of fellow humans to make themselves at home.

Contents

Introduction to My Hospitality Story 1

Descriptions and Reflections Upon
the Experience of Hospitality 23

Cultural Analysis 47

Welcome 65

Make Yourself at Home 79

Rest 89

Being Yourself 103

Conclusion 115

ACKNOWLEDGMENTS 121
ABOUT THE AUTHOR 123

– 1 –

Introduction to My Hospitality Story

Picture a woman gently, tenderly, and affectionately rubbing her pregnant belly. Inside Kathleen (Becrelis) Bilotta's womb, a baby is resting in its shelter, its home, feeling the warm, welcoming hospitality being extended by this woman affectionately known as Kitty.

Her husband, Vincent M. Bilotta, Jr., had used his Veterans Administration educational benefits to study plastics engineering in Los Angeles, California. The couple had married on March 6, 1946, and when Kitty was pregnant, in the early fall, she decided she wanted to give birth to her baby back home in the small New England city of Leominster, Massachusetts.

On February 2, 1947, a son was born to them. That son was me, Vincent M. Bilotta III. I was born into an Italian, Greek, and French-Canadian family.

"Junior," as my father was known, wanted his first son to carry his name, as he carried his father's name. While no fireworks were set off in the cold wintery sky that day, I imagine I felt embraced and welcomed.

For the first nine months of my life, we lived with my maternal grandparents, George and Marion (LaPrade) Becrelis, whom I came to know as Mémé and Pépé in their home, a bungalow in the Arts and Crafts style, built in 1930 at 42 Academy Road in Leominster. Our next stop was 53 Johnson Street. We lived in what was referred to as "the block," a neat, clean apartment building that housed six families, two on each floor.

Aunt Sunny and Uncle Wilfred

My father, mother, and I lived on the second floor, across the porch from my paternal Aunt Sunny and Uncle Wilfred. Aunt Sunny was a petite, slender, wonderfully vivacious, and fun-loving woman. My auntie had an infectious cheerful and energetic passion for life. Fearlessness of spirit was another of her gifts.

Unconditional love characterized her style. She was warm-hearted, accepting of herself, her family, and her extended family. She lived what she believed and said—politely—what was on her mind all the time.

Positive, optimistic, and nonjudgmental, gossiping or talking about others were not part of her style. Aunt Sunny had an unwavering faith in herself, others, and her God. She knew people were imperfect and believed it was important to be forgiving as soon as you could.

Having her priorities straight, she was not intimidated by wealth or materialism. She trusted that if you had your health, you were a very rich person and had everything.

I imagine the Corporal and Spiritual Works of Mercy, articles of the Roman Catholic faith, were important to Aunt Sunny because she lived her life by them. She was patient, kind, caring, gentle, and compassionate.

While working hard was part of her make up and she was always busy, she made sure that she was never too busy for her loved ones.

Everyone came to her house for coffee, conversation, and something to eat. She was a talented Italian cook, and her small kitchen was constantly filled with delicious aromas of her homemade tomato sauce or Italian cookies and cakes.

Aunt Sunny was an amazing woman and a good listener. She revered nature and wildlife, feeding the birds she saw as *her* birds.

In the afternoon, she enjoyed playing the music of her favorite Italian singers, Perry Como, Tony Bennett, and Frank Sinatra on her Victrola. She loved to sing and dance, and in her later years, she taught herself to play the guitar. She was, indeed, a woman who was able to sing her song and dance her dance.

Aunt Sunny was comforting and comfortable. She was like a blazing fireplace around which you could warm yourself, breathe deeply, feel at home, rest, and be yourself.

Uncle Wilfred was a strong man who worked out every day in his gym in the cellar of the block. Tarzan was his role model. A good swimmer, in his lifetime he saved two people from drowning. One rescue was in the Atlantic Ocean, off the coast of Maine, and the other was in a local lake.

People knew him to be an honest, genuine human being. He came across as down-to-earth while pulsating with a vigorous liveliness. You could count on him as a loyal person who would stand up for you.

A battle-hardened infantry soldier in World War II, he suffered from undiagnosed Post-Traumatic Stress Disorder. He had recurrent nightmares, depression, anxiety, and flashbacks to his war experiences. He was very sensitive to loud noises.

As he aged, he would have been described as exciting, wild, tough, and irreverent. Very colorful, he was a good storyteller who could entertain you with tales about the people, events, and escapades of his life.

A defender of the poor, the misunderstood, and the oppressed, he was a real friend to the little guy in town.

My uncle Wilfred was an officer with the Leominster Police Department, endearingly known as "the Sarge." When he came home from his 11:00 p.m. to 7:00 a.m. shift as the desk sergeant, he would knock on our door and ask my mother if "little Vinnie" could come over for breakfast with him and Aunt Sunny.

I happily took my place at their kitchen table. I would listen to the Sarge give the morning report of what happened the night before in the city. From two to four years old, despite not understanding what he was talking about, I felt secure that the Sarge was home and guarding our block. Sunny and Wilfred felt like my second parents.

Across the street from the block, Uncle Wilfred owned a piece of land nearly the size of a football field. After breakfast, he would invite me to be his little sidekick, helping him feed his animals that lived in a barn on the field. The pig, rabbits, chickens, and a horse were very excited to see us each morning. As we gave them fresh water and brought each their special feed, their various sounds seemed to express both a welcome to their barn and an excitement that they were being taken care of after the long night.

I so loved my Uncle Wilfred. A strong, masculine man, he patiently and kindly welcomed me into his male world. He was a powerful, wild, and crazy man, impressive in his size and bearing. He had many guns in his cellar and was ready to defend his family and his land at any moment. He taught me how to shoot a gun, box, explore nature, and respect all people.

Despite his bluster, Uncle Wilfred was kind to his animals and to people who were underdogs. The Sarge had an enormous warm, responsive, and gentle heart. A man concerned about peace and justice for all people, he was sensitive to the prejudice shown to working-class Italians in town, particularly by the Irish, the Protestants, and the many factory owners. Various gang leaders in town respected him because they knew he was sympathetic to their struggle as boys becoming men. He tried to keep rebellious juveniles out of jail. He was a good person with a strong work ethic. A humane individual, he was always polite and treated people with respect. He had a sense of what was right and wrong, good and bad. A down-to-earth person, he told it like it was.

Uncle Wilfred's personal suffering formed and shaped his sensitive heart. He believed all people should be treated with respect and he particularly strove to welcome the stranger, the rebellious, unconventional, unmanageable outsider, the misfit.

He provided work for them keeping up his various housing properties. When he died, the city's underdogs, former juvenile delinquents, alcoholics in and out of recovery came to pay their respects to this man who had struggled with the hypocrisy he saw in the city's upper echelon.

As a childhood friend of the Sarge said, "He was a very colorful, crazy, adventurous, and daring man, who was seemingly not afraid of anything or of saying anything that came to his mind."

My Uncle Wilfred stood out for me as a man who protected me and taught me powerful skills for life. He filled me with a soulfulness and an intense sensitivity to others in their struggle to survive in a very broken world.

My Father

Uncle Wilfred loved my father. Boyhood friends, they enjoyed each other's company as adults. They were *goombas*, the Italian term for close friends. He was very protective of my father as he struggled in the machine shops in Leominster. My father was a gifted machinist and tool and die maker. Uncle Wilfred would always praise my father in front of me, saying that he was a very smart man and would someday become a very successful plastics engineer.

Middle Street was an Italian-American working-class neighborhood where many of our relatives lived. My dad and I often would visit them and the neighbors along the street. They were very expressive with hugs and kisses as they welcomed us into their homes. Their immediate greeting would be, "Come, sit down at the kitchen table." Then they would ask if we wanted coffee, soda, or water. This was followed by a plate of anise-flavored Italian cookies with white frosting and sprinkles or jimmies, as Nonna called them. I loved the slight licorice or almond flavor of the cookies.

Nonna

My Italian grandmother, Nonna—Victoria (Faticanti) Bilotta—lived a quarter of a mile up the street. Nonna's husband died in 1943, when he was forty-nine years old, and Nonna became the matriarch of this large Italian-American family.

She was a tough cookie. A strong, powerful independent, Italian immigrant woman, she had a commanding presence. There were no pretenses. What you saw was what you got. She did not mince words. She told you who she liked and didn't like. If she did not like you, she would not open her door. She would tell you to go away or go home. She would make expressive faces about people she did not like. She walked with a limp caused by a fall down some stairs in a factory accident. To stabilize her gait, she used a *bastone*, the Italian word for cane. Being overweight increased her difficulty walking but did not interfere in her ability to rule the roost.

Nonna had the eyes of an eagle, and she would not let anyone in her presence get away with anything. One of her famous expressions was: "Watch out! I'm going to get my *bastone*."

At the same time, she could be gentle, kind, generous, and tenderhearted toward anyone she liked who walked onto her property or into her kitchen, especially her grandchildren. Most of the time she had a big smile and wide-open eyes. She was acutely present in the moment. On Sunday mornings, her house was filled with the sound of Italian opera. This ritual added to her soulfulness and delight in being alive.

Nonna was a woman with a mission: to care for and protect her family. She was a masterful cook and baker as well as a productive knitter and crocheter. Her vegetable and flower gardens were her pride and joy. Every spring she had a truckload of manure dumped in her driveway. She would recruit all the able-bodied people she knew to help her feed her garden with the beautiful, rich organic material. Her gladiolas, pansies, petunias, and geraniums thrived with this wonderful contribution to the soil. Over the summer, the cherry, peach, and pear trees would gradually respond with a great abundance of fruit.

My Nonna was always good to me. Her smile melted me. She always seemed to be standing at her stove, stirring a large pot of delightfully seasoned tomato/meat sauce for her homemade macaroni, lasagna, eggplant parmigiana, or ravioli.

If Nonna liked you and you were family, she would warmly welcome you into her home. At times, she could not contain her excitement. Eager to share whatever she had with those she loved, she always looked forward to a visit. A table, some chairs, some food, and conversation comforted all our souls as we all continued to fight the good fight, to lift up our hearts, and rejoice that we had each other. In those moments, we knew that all would be well.

The Gifts of Being Welcomed

In his book, *Setting the Table*[1], Danny Meyer writes: "Within moments of being born, most babies find themselves receiving the first four gifts of life:

---

1 Meyer, Danny, *Setting the Table*. New York: Harper (2006) p. 10

eye contact, a smile, a hug, and some food. We receive many other gifts in life, but few could ever surpass those first four. That first time may be the purest 'hospitality interaction' we will ever have, and it is not much of a surprise that we will crave those gifts for the rest of our lives. I know I do."

In this quote, we get a quick glimpse not only of hospitality, but a wonderful statement about the experience of being welcomed. I remember so well being welcomed time after time by my Italian grandmother, aunts, uncles, and other relatives. Eye contact, a smile, a hug, and some food were all part of the welcome, but it seemed a lot more than that. I realize now that when I walked into their presence, I was greeted with excitement, aliveness, recognition, and affirmation. I felt safe, secure, accepted, supported, and free to be myself. I was nurtured, nourished, loved, centered, and grounded. I felt respected, energized, revered, and potent. This was quite a gift to receive in an ongoing way, during my tender, formative years. I would knock on a door, and someone would shout and proclaim my name, "Vincent!" It felt like a prince had arrived—he is here! The greeters, the welcomers would immediately say that it was so wonderful that I was in their midst. I felt, anointed, blessed, confirmed, and warmly, tenderly received.

I always knew I was a good boy, and people liked me. I was my father's first child, his first son. I felt that I was special, but I also sensed these relatives were deeply interested in me and how I was progressing in my life. Many of these people never graduated from grammar school, never mind experiencing any higher education, but they all had hopes and dreams for me. Over the years, they lovingly expressed their concerns for me as I grew from a boy to a man under their watchful, caring gazes.

When I say I felt special, it was not that I was the most important person in the extended family. My being was good enough. This was so impactful upon my development that I never questioned my intrinsic goodness. My essential nature was that I was a good person.

None of this means that I did not misbehave or drive my mother nuts at times. I just never found myself—and never have found myself—questioning my essential goodness. I was anointed by my extended Italian family as good and this confirmation from my tribe filled my heart and soul. It became part of who I was, and how I continued to experience myself to be.

I internalized over and over this feeling of being a good person. It was gently impressed upon me in what seemed to be an ongoing sacred ritual. They all continued to speak well of me. This created in me a belief that my being was good enough and that I belonged to the tribe.

My experience of hospitality from my Italian relatives is a powerful example of what a community of people, events, and things can give to a kid. It forms and shapes his life forever. I have been hosted and welcomed well. I was given space and time to feel—and be—at home. Their hospitality gave me a sense of at-homeness both within their homes and within me.

I find myself welling up with deep gratitude that expands my heart as I remember how I was embraced by my relatives on Middle Street. Their style of hospitality formed and shaped in me a disposition to be kind to myself and others in my everyday life. I was explicitly invited and received into this world with warm acceptance and kind affection. I am very grateful for the great bountiful gift of the mystery of this powerful blessing.

I have described how my Italian-American family lived out their tradition of hospitality as I grew and prospered from boyhood to manhood. With all their distinct personalities, it was the tradition that mattered. Other parts of my extended family were Greek and French-Canadian in origin. They, too, brought their own hospitality traditions to bear upon me in ways that continue to shape and form me today.

Wally and His Family

Wally, one of my childhood friends, shared a story about his Aunt Ruth, who was married to Amerigo, brother of his mother, Gracie. Ruth was a plain woman who radiated an internal beauty. Soft-spoken, nonjudgmental, kind, and concerned, she lived the virtues of hard work, thriftiness, and self-discipline. She had a natural, free-flowing energy. She was neither rigid nor dogmatic in her beliefs.

Ruth came from the city's upper middle class. Her father was vice president of one of the local banks. Shaped and formed in the Protestant-Unitarian tradition, she valued individual freedom of belief, the free use of reason in religion, a united world community, and liberal social action. She had a calm demeanor, which was the polar opposite of the Italian-American working class family she joined in marrying Amerigo.

As a young woman, Ruth served in the Women's Army Corps. She went to college under the GI Bill and graduated with a master's degree in Child Development and Education from Columbia University.

Her husband, Amerigo, was an eccentric man. He was prone to invent stories about exploits everyone completely understood had little grounding in reality.

In the 1930s, Amerigo had been a star half-back on his high school football team. Whenever he told one of his clearly fantastic stories, his mother, Germania, would tap his forehead, say in her broken English, "too *mucha futaballa.*" This was decades before anyone was talking about the impact concussion might have on football players' brains.

One of the Amerigo stories Wally shared was about a day in late May when he showed up boasting to his brother, Peter, that he already had bright red, plump tomatoes in his vegetable garden. "Ripe tomatoes in a New England backyard garden in May?" Peter asked, adding that Amerigo was crazy, making up another story.

Uncle Amerigo replied: "If you don't believe me, get into my car and come and see them for yourself in my garden." Off they went.

When they arrived at Amerigo's garden, he said, "Look!" And there, on each tomato plant, were beautiful tomatoes hanging from the vines in the sunlight. Peter was in disbelief.

When Ruth called Amerigo into their house for a minute, Uncle Peter, still flabbergasted, unlocked the steel gate to investigate further. He carefully leaned down toward the plants and saw that Amerigo had delicately attached what clearly were store-bought tomatoes to the vines of the plants. Some tomatoes still had the little sticker from the store on them!

Just then, Amerigo came out of the house, exclaiming: "Isn't it amazing!"

Peter looked at his unpredictable, unrestrained brother and said he was really an odd duck. He embraced Amerigo, a character who lived as a trickster. "You will never change. You always amaze me, but I love you!" Peter told Amerigo. "You are my brother."

Wally's Uncle Peter was a boyhood friend of my father and Uncle Wilfred. They were all *goombas*. He was exuberant as a child, young man, and as an old man. Peter exhibited a great love of life and pure joy at being with other people. He especially doted on his many nieces and nephews, as well as his own daughter, Pattie. He loved to cook and invite his extended family and friends over for breakfast, lunch, or dinner. Each meal was a labor of love and an enthusiastic celebration of the gift of food and the act of breaking bread. I remember hearing Uncle Peter say: "Try this bread. It will drive you crazy. Oh my God!" Uncle Peter's use of exaggeration was indicative of his desire for you to enjoy the moment.

When Uncle Peter was eating, he would keep his eyes closed. He so wanted to enjoy the food he was consuming that he did not want any other sensations to interfere. He would block out the world for a moment. He would close his eyes as if he was concentrating on receiving Holy Communion. Eating was a sacramental moment.

Another tall tale of Uncle Amerigo's whimsical imagination centered on fishing, a sport he enjoyed. He told a yarn about discovering a pond on the border between Massachusetts and New Hampshire that he swore nobody knew except him. It was his own special place, filled with extraordinary fish. In this enchanting place, he had to go behind a tree to bait his pole because if the fish caught sight of the worm, they would start jumping out of the pond. Hearing this fish story all their lives, Amerigo's sons had fish leaping out of a lake engraved on his tombstone in the Evergreen Cemetery in Leominster.

Amerigo's wife, Ruth, became a teacher at Lancaster Street School, where my friend Wally attended grammar school. Through his formative years, his Aunt Ruth passed on her love of reading to Wally, especially American literature. The world of great literature provided Wally with a welcome refuge from the playing fields that were filled with more accomplished athletes.

Wally's father, a talented carpenter, built a screened-in back porch that overlooked an enormous vegetable garden. A well-kept lawn stretched from the back porch to the stone wall that acted as a border between Wally's house at 170 Lancaster Street and a productive acreage of vegetable plants.

Wally and I shared a similar background of growing up in white working-class, Italian, Catholic families. Our parents were not intellectually engaged and did not delight in the pleasure of reading.

Like our parents, Wally and I were childhood friends. He likes to tell the story that he and I were born at the same hospital, three months apart. When we were seven, we became altar boys together.

In 1962, my house was very loud and noisy. At that time my parents and nine children filled our small three-bedroom ranch house and shared one bathroom. A long picnic table was our dining room table as well as the place where we did homework.

Wally, the older of two boys, enjoyed coming over for dinner and interacting with my family. We both studied at the public library, a gracious old building.

One Saturday afternoon in July 1962, Wally invited me to sit on his quiet back porch and read. There, as I was going into my junior year of high school, I discovered the pleasure of reading.

The first book I read in this new formative discipline was *The Art of Loving*[2] by Erich Fromm. The back story behind this choice was that I was beginning to fall in love with my first real girlfriend. Insecure and feeling inferior, I went to the local library, looked through the index cards about the topic of love, and discovered Fromm's book.

So, there we were, Wally reading his American literature book and me my *Art of Loving*[2]. Wally's mother, Gracie, brought us milk and Italian cookies.

A real character, Gracie was socially active, a no-nonsense, lively woman who was very expressive. She engaged with you in a way that was uplifting to your spirit but was never intrusive.

Coming from a poor Italian family, she suffered a lot but had a sense of humor that was grounding and helped you to grow in humility. That is, knowing your place in the world and not taking it all too seriously.

I felt Gracie was always rooting for us. As playful as she could be, she had a sense that what we were doing on her porch those Saturdays in the summer of 1962 was really important for our futures. She knew that

---

2 Fromm, Erich. The Art of Loving. New York: HarperCollins (2000)

reading would be a pathway to higher education—a possible ticket to a better life than hers.

My Fromm book posed the question: What does it mean to be human? This became the most fundamental and important question in my life. It became the theme of the journey of my entire life.

On the porch "existential" became my word. *The Art of Loving* drew me to my second book: Victor Frankl's *Man's Search for Meaning*[3], which I devoured that summer. Looking back, I can see the flow of my philosophical curiosity. The journey of exploring, "What's it all about?" was a mystery and a gift. What is the meaning of life? How should I live my life? Who will help me become reflective about my life and seek a path to wisdom?

Recalling my exposure to the art of reading and the search for formative direction for my life, I realized that Fromm, Frankl, and others called on me to participate in a reflective journey to uncover, discover, and understand what it means to be human in its most developed sense.

In his book, *12 Rules for Life: An Antidote to Chaos*[4], Jordon B. Peterson writes, "If you are reading this book there is a strong possibility that you are a privileged person. You can read. You've perched high in the clouds. It took untold generations to get you where you are. A little gratitude may be in order."

Looking back on that scene of the screened-in porch, I find myself grateful to Wally for his introduction to the art of reading and the pursuit of knowledge. Reading has indeed been a privilege and a pleasure. I also am grateful to all my relatives and friends who cheered me on to go to college and to fulfill my desire to try to understand what it means to be human.

Holy Cross

On September 21, 1964, I began my college studies at Holy Cross, then a small men's liberal arts college in Worcester, Massachusetts. Its strong humanistic approach deepened in me a love of the pursuit of knowledge.

---

3 Frankl, Victor. *Man's Search for Meaning*. Boston: Beacon Press (2006)
4 Peterson, Jordon B. *12 Rules for Life: An Antidote for Chaos*. New York: Penguin. (2019) p. 242

I was called to become a reflective citizen and to develop a respect for my fellow man and to become a man for others.

In learning to think creatively and critically, I was encouraged to explore a search for the holy through a wholistic approach of pursuing a wholeness of mind, body, and spirit. Fundamental religious and philosophical questions were raised as a method to help me find meaning in my life and in history. It helped me to make more explicit what was implicit in my experience, to probe and question whatever is discussed, and not take things at face value. I am grateful that I learned how to think, communicate, and to express myself through the written word.

Through its interdisciplinary approach, The Cross facilitated a process in me of wanting to serve others—and in fact, to change the world. I developed a desire to serve others by giving back. I was being formed to become a cultural change agent.

There I was, at the bottom of Wheeler Hall, a six-story, brown-orange clay colored brick structure built in 1940. On Thursday, September 24, 1964, at 8:00 a.m., I took my seat in my first class at the college. The professor, a Jesuit priest, dressed in a black cassock, a long plain black garment traditionally worn by the religious order, walked into our Rational Philosophy class and wrote this question on the blackboard: What does it mean to be human? He repeated in a serious tone: What does it mean to be human? Since that moment in my seventeenth year of life, that question has been my guiding question for all my adult life. I am now seventy-five years old and it has been fifty-eight years since I was challenged by this profound, but essential question.

I had the good fortune of having Paul S. Rosenkrantz, Ph.D., assigned as my academic advisor. Walking into the first floor of Alumni Hall where the psychology professors had their offices, I knocked on the door and a pleasant, soft-spoken voice invited me into the office.

There Dr. Rosenkrantz sat comfortably in his old wooden swivel chair, wearing a tweed jacket with leather patches on the elbows. A Jewish immigrant from Eastern Europe, his wrinkled face told a story of having been through a lot. His warm inviting smile was cheery and uplifting. As I sat down in his visitor's chair, he started his ritual of packing the bowl of his pipe with the wonderfully aromatic George Washington Cherry Tobacco. I was familiar with the scent because it was the tobacco my Greek immigrant maternal grandfather used in his pipes.

There I was, a newly minted college freshman, sitting with this wise old gentleman. His desk was piled with books, papers, and journals. During our conversation, I shared with him my interest in Fromm and Frankl and the Existential Psychology movement.

At the time, I did not know that Dr. Rosenkrantz had received his doctorate in clinical psychology at Clark University across town in Worcester. I later came to understand that he had taken courses on Existential Psychology. That way of thinking was part of a thread that influenced the Department of Psychology at that time.

When I told him about my interest in Existential Psychology, his first question to me was: "What do you want to do with the rest of your life?"

My response was that my classmates in high school often said I was a good listener and that I should think of becoming a counselor. This was why I wanted to declare psychology as my major.

In his wisdom, Dr. Rosenkrantz told me if I wanted to become a psychologist, I should major in philosophy. I was surprised by his suggestion but followed his advice. Although I officially graduated as a philosophy major, I had enough credits to qualify as a psychology major, too. This enabled me to go on to graduate school to pursue a doctorate in psychology.

In this supportive and effective learning environment at Holy Cross, I felt engaged in a creative dialogue with Dr. Rosenkrantz. He inspired me to pursue my dream of becoming a psychotherapist.

Looking back, it was such a blessing, a graced circumstance that the Department of Philosophy had gathered a number of faculty members who considered themselves Existential Phenomenologists. It was this perspective, this approach, this manner of thinking that began with embracing human experience. The phenomena to study were human experience, not just human behavior, human action, or reaction to stimulation. The focus was to become awake, aware, alert, and attentive to what we are noticing, experiencing, sensing that which is before us, around us, inside us. This approach would help me become grounded in the study of everyday life experience. It taught me to explore human nature and helped me become more compassionate, human, and humane in my own life.

Another fortunate coincidence occurred at Holy Cross. It was a tradition that every freshman was assigned a member of the senior class who acted as a "big brother." As the oldest of eleven children, I had never had a big brother. I felt comforted to have a senior available to me as I faced the sometimes overwhelming transition to college life.

Again, a moment of grace seemed to emerge in the lobby of O'Kane Hall as my senior student advisor leaned toward me and spoke about the conflict going on in Southeast Asia, Vietnam, to be exact. My advisor, who was in the Air Force Reserve Officers Training Corps, suggested that I consider enrolling in the college's Air Force ROTC detachment. He put it this way: "It sounds like you want to become a psychologist and you're headed to graduate school." The Air Force needs psychologists to help people coming back from conflicts like Vietnam, he said. "Join now. Stay in for your freshman and sophomore years. Come your junior year, see where this Vietnam conflict is. You could drop out then or move on to graduate as an officer," he advised. Part of the context of this important conversation is that I came to learn that the Air Force was very committed to higher education.

At graduation in spring 1968, it was clear that only men continuing on to medical school were being given deferments from their local draft boards. Had I not accepted my commission to become an officer in the Air Force, I most likely would have been drafted into some branch of the United States Armed Forces. Anticipating a great need for trained clinical therapists to work with service men and women returning from Vietnam, the Air Force granted me a deferment to continue my studies in a doctoral program. I enrolled at Duquesne University in Pittsburgh, Pennsylvania, in the fall of 1968. In 1972, having completed my coursework, I reported for duty in San Antonio, Texas, the first post of my four-year commitment to the Air Force.

My Quest to Understand Hospitality

After my service with the Air Force, the completion of my dissertation, and the awarding of my doctoral degree, my work led me to consult with clergy and religious in the Catholic Church for more than fifty years. I read and studied the mission, vision, and values of these organizations. In the course of my work, I came to offer a sabbatical program for clergy and religious. One participant was a nun from the Sisters of the Hospitallers. Their history dates to the twelfth century and the Crusades. Their founding purpose was to provide hospitality to the Crusaders and pilgrims who were traveling back and forth from Europe to Jerusalem in the Middle East. In reading their mission, vision, and value statements, it was clear that they provided food and lodging for people on the pilgrimage to the Holy Lands.

I was disappointed at the lack of articulation of their understanding of the true nature of hospitality—what it is, how it manifests, and how it affects human beings?

I presumed that this ancient religious order would be able to provide me with a deep understanding of the powerful human experience of hospitality. Providing food and lodging, although great corporal works of mercy, was not what I was looking for. My hope was they could offer me a more explicit articulation of the phenomenon of hospitality. That did not happen.

What did happen was that I was deeply touched by the word, the experience, the phenomenon of hospitality. My work with these nuns began to help me see and appreciate my own experience of hospitality.

I remember a film I viewed at Holy Cross in 1966, an avant-garde cultural piece titled, *Blow Up*[5], directed by Michelangelo Antonioni. Set in London, in the 1960s, the story was about a peaceful lush garden park where a man was murdered.

A photographer taking pictures of the grand park's landscape said that the light in the park was very good. Developing the negatives of his shoot later, he realized he had inadvertently captured a murder. Behind a waist-high, old, worn, shrub-covered picket fence, there was a face in the bushes.

As he blew up the pictures, he saw more of the story unfold. There was a man with a rifle who killed the man in the park. The magnification of the pictures made the murder more explicit.

Across time and space, human beings have been involved with the

---

5 Antonioni, Michelangelo, dir. *Blow-Up*. 1966 Criterion

everyday life experience of hospitality. How can we blow up this picture, this experience, and make more explicit what is implicit in this behavior, this moment, this human gesture that we call hospitality?

You know it when you see it, when you experience it. You are grateful when you experience it. It gives you comfort and helps you to sink deeper into the moment.

What is this experience? There are many books on the topic. Major universities have departments, colleges, and specialized schools devoted to this phenomenon. The perspective presented is typically one from a behavioral, functional stance. Such programs are devoted to the *behavior* of hospitality.

Hospitality as Big Business

Hospitality is a major industry in this country and around the world. But what is it and what does it provide? It seems to be about food and lodging and is typically associated with tourism.

The Hospitallers provided food and lodging for the Crusaders in the twelfth century. From kings in their palaces to indigenous people in their huts, teepees, and caves, it is the practice, the gesture of hospitality according to the customs of each. It is a dynamic that has been practiced over and over every day since the beginning of human interpersonal interaction.

Hospitality matters! It is important and significant. The hospitality industry is a multibillion-dollar business that has branded a certain understanding of the concept. It has been commodified. That means that it has become part of the capitalistic economic consumer system in which everything is to be sold, bought, and consumed. Mass media, agencies of mass communication, serve as medium cultivating, conveying, and expressing this process of commodification. The perspective is from the angle of making everything possible into a mere product to be sold, bought, and consumed.

Commercialized, hospitality has become a big business. The hospitality industry has emphasized the utility of the product, its worth, purpose, and goal. To yield results, benefits, and profits, the industry is devoted to anticipating the wants and needs as well as the desires of the customer. Success is realized in pleasing the customer within those parameters.

The hospitality industry is a broad category of fields within the service industry that includes the following four segments: food and beverages; leisure; travel and tourism; lodging and recreation. All of that is what is associated with the word hospitality in the industry, the business of hospitality.

Hospitality as a Human Experience

But there is another vein, aspect, association with the word hospitality. This would be viewing hospitality as a human experience. The question then becomes: what is the experience of hospitality? What are the aspects, dimensions, the particulars of the human phenomenon? What is its essential structure, its essence as a human experience?

Hospitality carries great worth, value, and consequence. It's a quality of life that shows itself by word, signal, and gesture. An element of being humane, it demonstrates an important dimension of what it means to be human. It is a graced quality of life, of superior worth.

Hospitality is a virtue. It is a habit of service, a mode of consciousness in our daily lives. The stranger becomes our brother and neighbor. The visitor is treated well as a favored, honored guest. The rule is to welcome the stranger with sympathy, kindness, profound respect, gentleness, reverence, and politeness. The guest is treated with care, willingness, and graciousness. The host receives the guest in a warm, friendly, and generous way. The hope is that the guest will experience a sense of peace in sharing space and time with the host.

The purpose of this book is to attempt to answer the questions:

- What is hospitality?
- What is the essence of hospitality?
- What does hospitality mean?

This book is a journey to seek, inquire, investigate, and examine this bountiful human experience. I will attempt to walk around it, observe it, describe the experience of it, analyze it, and articulate the what of hospitality.

My goal is to attain a tangible understanding of the phenomenon of hospitality. To do so I will use an existential phenomenological approach. I will elucidate and describe the dynamics and structure of hospitality by using a qualitative methodology rather than a quantitative approach.

A qualitative approach is designed to identify the components, the characteristics of hospitality. It is focused on the particular and the essential character, the inherent distinct traits or characteristics that belong to the nature of the lived, human experience of hospitality.

As an example, in the references to the many characters in my early life, mother, father, Sunny, Wilfred, and others, there is a host and a guest, a welcomer and a visitor. Host and visitor components are constituents of the experience of hospitality.

Other guiding questions that contribute to the understanding of hospitality would be:

- How is the phenomenon of hospitality lived out, arranged in a definite pattern of organization?
- How are its aggregate of elements, constituents arranged, constructed in a specific manner in their relationship to each other?

My hope is that the methodology of existential phenomenology will provide a rigorous, disciplined, and systematic approach to help me to describe and reflect in a specific manner on the experience of hospitality. My intent is to shed light on the unfolding structure of the human experience of hospitality. I intend to articulate a new, unique definition of this important phenomenon.

Let us go back to the story of the photographer in the Grand Park in London. By blowing up the negative, enhancing the magnitude of the pixels that together constitute the image of the photograph, the photographer was able to see a figure with a rifle hiding in the bushes. The blow-up, the magnifying, the enhancing enabled the photographer to see more clearly what was there in the picture. We could say that he made the implicit more explicit, the invisible, visible.

The perspective of existential phenomenology emphasizes individual human experience that includes being grounded in space, time, the human body, self, other, and culture. This means that any description of a human experience would contain, as part of the whole, the above mentioned existentialia. These general constituent components or elements will be found as part of the articulation of the phenomenon of hospitality. These various aspects of human experience act as a framing post, as pieces of the gestalt, the pieces that make up the whole of any human phenomenon. Identifying these threads, these particulars, and articulating them will help us make explicit what is implicit in the essential structure, essence, quiddity of hospitality.

Looking at some of my experiences of hospitality—the situations, the cast of characters, scenes as in a play, lines in the script—helps distinguish commercialized hospitality and the breadth and depth of the bounty of hospitality as it is being lived out in everyday life.

Hospitality can become a countercultural response to the need to change the culture. Greed, rudeness, and corruption have had and continue to have significant influence on the unfolding of the culture. The commercialization of hospitality for financial gain has damaged the culture and debased the dignity of the person.

Hospitality is a mode of consciousness. It is a complete moral, emotional, intellectual, and civic way of being. It is a way of seeing the other and the world. It is a progressive development of our internal consciousness.

From this perspective of hospitality as a mode of consciousness, we begin to see ourselves and others in our relationships to the wider world from a certain lens. It is this view that the other is my neighbor and it is up to each of us to grow into a way of being that we lead with our hands open, with inviting eyes, sensitive ears, and a warm heart. As the Benedictines[6] would say, the stranger is the visitor, the guest is another Christ.

This powerful human disposition, this attitude of hospitality, can improve our lives. It can become an effective solution to the cultural problems of incivility, disrespect, and lack of dignity.

---

6 Saint Benedict's Rule for Monasteries. Collegeville, MN (1948) Chapter 53 p. 72-74

I am interested in making a small contribution to the unfolding of the culture. In picking up the mantle, the pen, the keyboard in writing this book, I continue my search for the answer to the question: What does it mean to be human? My hunch is that an understanding of hospitality will help me become a better cultural change agent by transforming me into a more humane human being. It is my hope that the spirit of cultural transformation will be expanded by a deeper understanding of the phenomenon of hospitality.

As Jordon B. Peterson pointed out, "It took untold generations to get you where you are!"[7] My experience with the characters, events, and things in my early life gave me a bounty of hospitality, and I am grateful. This sense of hospitality has grounded me, given me a center, a space, a place from which to emerge and unfold as a man concerned for others.

All these people had their doors open, hands out, eyes welcoming, voices exclaiming: "Welcome! Make yourself at home in order to rest and be yourself." They helped form my personality and character. Through their hospitality, they leaned in and gave me direction for my everyday life. They whispered and witnessed in their words and gestures that the kitchen table was available to sit, abide, dwell, and be with them. In this connection around the kitchen table, they were hosts who gave me hospitality and treated me as a precious, fragile, vulnerable human being who was sacred and perceived as Christ.

As a young altar boy, I served Mass when assigned. After the service, I would find my way to some relative on Middle Street. I would knock on the door and be invited in to join the gathering crowd around the kitchen table. There I would feel warmth, respect and reverence. I was a member of their tribe, and I was invited to take my place as a guest at the table, and join in by listening, observing, and participating in their lively offering of hospitality.

When I would show up at the door of a family member or close friends of our family, I would be immediately greeted with eye contact, a smile,

---

7 Ibid, Peterson, p. 242

a hug, and some food. The atmosphere around the kitchen table would be filled with care, concern, and generosity. A place would be set for me. They would make room for me at the table. They valued my presence. I was Vinnie, my father's son. I felt their warmth, honor, and respect. I was now the sacred guest, welcomed into the circle around the table.

— 2 —

Descriptions and Reflections Upon the Experience of Hospitality

My understanding of the experience of hospitality needed to be grounded in everyday life descriptions of hospitality. In this chapter, I will share with you detailed, elaborate accounts of experiences of hospitality.

Over time, I gathered more than 300 descriptions of hospitality from people who were able to locate a time, an event, a situation where hospitality emerged for them. Although I learned something about hospitality, the descriptions lacked depth and breadth.

Eventually, I decided I would give it a try myself. The first people who came to mind were Mémé, Nonna, and Julie Country Day School. These were people and spaces with whom and where I powerfully felt a sense of hospitality. The question emerged: Why these? What made these experiences leap out at me? What was it about them that my mind and body were immediately flooded with thoughts and feelings of welcome, comfort, and at-homeness?

Mémé and Pépé, Nonna, and Julie Country Day each had a story in my life. Each had a specific address in the city of Leominster, Massachusetts: 42 Academy Road, 53 Middle Street, and 401 Lindell Avenue. I experienced hospitality there.

My task would be to describe what made these spaces hospitable for me. Even as I recalled these addresses, I experienced a sense of peace, comfort, and joy. What happened at these addresses?

Mémé and Pépé's house introduced me to the Arts and Crafts movement.

My studies later introduced me to William Morris, who founded the movement in Britain and to Gustav Stickley, who later established it in America.

In reading about Arts and Crafts houses and what they were trying to experientially orchestrate for residents, I said to myself that is exactly what I experienced in Mémé and Pépé's house at 42 Academy Road. For a while, I was all caught up in the design of the house and in believing it was the design that facilitated the experience of hospitality. Upon further reflection, I acknowledged that it was not just the house design but great hosts who continually invited me, welcomed me, and just let me be myself in their home.

At 53 Middle Street, I would make a simple knock on the back door and hear my Nonna yell: "Come in!" I would experience a rush of thoughts, feelings, and sensations at being welcomed to her kitchen table for coffee, food, and conversation.

At 401 Lindell Avenue, the Julie Country Day estate, I was invited into a beautiful English-style botanical garden. Each time I set my foot on this land, I felt awe, wonder, and mystery in this place of tranquility and pastoral peacefulness.

Initially these were unfolding bodily experiences. Over time, I have found the words to describe these experiences of hospitality.

As part of the process of describing hospitality in these spaces, I interviewed at length my aunts, uncles, friends, and neighbors as well as my brothers and sisters about their experiences in these places.

As a psychotherapist, another part of this process was preparing a Family of Origin Seminar for my company, Formation Consultation Services through which I provided ongoing formation consulting to religious orders in the United States, Europe, Central America, Australia, and the Caribbean Islands. This preparation provided me an opportunity to abide and dwell in these experiences of hospitality from a family of origin perspective.

As background to enhance understanding of the three properties upon which I reflected as core experiences of hospitality, I also researched the archives of the Leominster Historical Society for information about 42

Academy Road (Mémé), 53 Middle Street (Nonna), and 401 Lindell Avenue (Julie Country Day estate).

Mémé

Mémé's plain, four-square Arts and Crafts style home was built in 1930 in Leominster, Massachusetts. This two-story, seven-room Colonial had bungalow pillars at the entry to its large screened-in front porch. The porch created an outdoor room. In front of the porch, mature arborvitae trees and bushes from the cypress family with red berries created an evergreen cave-like atmosphere. It was always shady on the porch. You could see out, but people could not see in through the closely overlapping, well-developed decorative arborvitae plantings.

The porch was more than the main entrance to the interior of the house. It was a cozy space with comfortable rocking chairs. From early spring to late fall, my maternal grandparents would sit and enjoy each other's company as they passed the time together.

William Morris originated the British Arts and Crafts movement in the late nineteenth century. His movement was a reaction against the Industrial Revolution's mechanization of human beings in which the human laborer became devalued, degraded, and disconnected from nature. To combat what he saw as industrialization murdering the human soul, Morris's movement honored the dignity of the human laborer and emphasized the workman as a craftsman with a relationship to his natural, organic material. Simplicity, honesty, and inherent beauty in the design was valued along with why and how things were made.

Gustav Stickley brought the spirit of William Morris's philosophy to America. He believed it was the hand of the man that counted. Attention to details called forth good workmanship, inspiring craftsmanship and appreciation of the dignity and value of good design. The useful, the beautiful, the simple, and the direct, all guided his creative efforts. He paused to give attention to the ordinary by making a tangible home for the soul by finding the sacred in everything including the wood grain, the colors of nature, and plant forms.

The dignified and substantial house at 42 Academy Road was built with fine materials and superb craftsmanship. In line with the spirit of English architect William Morris and American architect Gustav Stickley, this house was a living space that fostered genuine, authentic graciousness. Its clear lines, unassuming materials, and simplification of design cultivated grace, beauty, and comfort. The handicraft of this structure was a product of individual expression. Its order, harmony, and reduction to basic essentials cultivated the care of the human soul and encouraged its inhabitants to do less, be leisurely, and behold more.

My maternal grandparents, George and Marion (LaPrade) Becrelis, who were Mémé and Pépé to me, moved into 42 Academy Road in 1944. My grandfather was a Greek immigrant, the oldest of six children, who possessed a firmness of mind and will. In 1899, at the tender age of twelve he came to America from Mytilene, the capital city of the Greek Island of Lesbos, to seek his fortune.

At this early age, George had already developed a strong work ethic. Energetic, steady, and earnest, he was interested in thriving, not surviving. With fortitude and resilience, his quiet, patient temperament enabled him to hold his own and keep up his morale to achieve his goals.

George was courageous, bold, and determined to succeed in America. At age twenty, he had the imagination and foresight to become his own boss and control his unfolding economic situation. In 1912, he became a small business owner. At twenty-five, he established, owned, and operated the Boston Confectionary Store and Restaurant at 44 Monument Square in the center of the city of Leominster, Massachusetts. His nascent entrepreneurship assisted him in becoming a successful proprietor. He guaranteed that his homemade confections, rich and flavorful ice cream, and salted nuts were pure and wholesome. He knew what his patrons wanted, and he worked hard to satisfy them. His practical judgment, acute perceptions about his customers, and his diplomatic skills, all contributed to his thriving business for forty years.

The Boston Confectionary Store and Restaurant was the local hangout for teenagers after school. It was also the favorite breakfast and lunch spot of community officials, storeowners, and their staffs. To this day, people remember his professionalism as a host, a greeter, and a welcomer who was especially cordial and friendly to his customers. His personal fulfillment came in his serving others. On Thanksgiving Day and Christmas Day, he would open his restaurant in the morning to make sure that people who were down and out had a meal for the day. After he closed his store in the late afternoon each day, he delivered food packages to the poor along his way home. His compassion and generosity to the needy emerged from his traditional Greek Orthodox religious values as well as his commitment to just being a man for serving others.

Mémé's French-Canadian ancestors, from Sorel, Quebec, about fifty miles north of Montreal, were hunters, fur traders, and farmers. Despite being persecuted and defeated by the English, her ancestors continued to farm. The use of antiquated farming implements and soil-depleting farm methods began to exhaust the soil, rendering it infertile in the mid-1800s. The stresses of possible crop blight, a shorter growing season from being so far north and subject to early frost, led to poor harvests and low crop prices. The farmers in this area of Quebec were unable to maintain viable farms and fell into debt.

Unemployed in this strained economy, Mémé's ancestors descended into poverty. They were vulnerable and ripe for recruitment by the New England mill owners who sent French-Canadian workers to Quebec to recruit more workers for their mills. Despite promises of heaven on earth, they were used and abused by the wool and cotton textile mill owners when they arrived in New England. They labored on their feet twelve hours a day in a very fast-paced, monotonous environment. The clamorous noise of the textile machines was deafening. Cotton dust choked their lungs. Many collapsed under the heat of the machines. The work was grinding, boring, and debilitating. The owners continued to tighten standards of discipline and productivity, demanding more production in less time. The workers were under constant strain and pressure to never make a mistake that would stop the machines. They feared that if the machines stopped, the enraged owners would fire them, plunging their families deeper into poverty.

The Frogs, Canucks, Frenchies—offensive terms for the French-Canadians—were resented by the Irish workers who came before them as interlopers who were willing to work in the mills and factories for lower wages. Docile, duty-bound, and loyal workers, the French-Canadians were neither overly energetic nor ambitious. They saw themselves as being in exile, surrounded by hostile people. They felt disheartened, unappreciated, and developed habits of resignation. They experienced disdain, prejudice, and discrimination as each group of newly arrived immigrants from other countries experienced.

Alcoholism permeated the lives of Mémé's father and several of her brothers. As a way of coping, she clung to her strict, rigid, and harsh Jansenist Roman Catholic religious culture. Marion married George Becrelis, who was Greek Orthodox, in 1917, which had the effect of saving her from the downward spiral that overcame many of her immediate family members. While the local Greek community did not immediately welcome her, she was accepted in time.

Marion, my Mémé, was quiet, shy, and uncomplaining. Carrying a sense of French-Canadian defeatism, she was a long-suffering human being with low self-esteem. She tended to worry, be anxious, and lacking belief in herself, felt inferior. While holding on for dear life, she was a hard worker who was persistent, enduring, and tenacious. As a wife and mother, she took on the responsibility of overseeing the family's welfare.

In 1930, my grandmother asked my Pépé if he would build a restaurant on a piece of land they owned in a town south of Leominster. Her father and three of her brothers were alcoholics. She thought one of these brothers who was a good professional cook could run the restaurant and that work would keep him sober.

An intensely family-oriented husband and father, George responded to his wife's request to fulfill his role as a provider and protector. Establishing another business gave George more meaning, purpose, and satisfaction. Within a year he built, established, owned, and operated the new Brier Rabbit Restaurant in the town of Sterling. My mother and her five sisters all worked as waitresses at both The Boston Confectionary Store and the Brier Rabbit restaurants as teenagers. They cultivated their culinary and hospitality skills as they contributed to the development of the family businesses.

While Mémé's feelings of inferiority and defeat ran deep, miraculously they brought her to a place of humility, not humiliation. She never became a puffed-up, arrogant, know-it-all. Married to George, staunch in her religion, she grew into understanding that she was a lovely creature of her God. Her family history of brokenness became her access to depend humbly on her God for care, support, and gratitude.

Despite her family history of depreciation and emotional deprivation, her home, the William Morris Arts and Crafts house where she and her husband lived at 42 Academy Road became the umbrella space for experiences of hospitality. William Morris's style was part of the backdrop that commingled with Mémé's French-Canadian simplicity to ultimately cultivate a powerful homeyness.

Mémé's life story and 42 Academy Road intertwined, creating an outstanding space of ordinary intimacy. This Arts and Crafts home became the horizon, the backdrop, part of the historical perspective of the use of space that was a marker event of a powerful experience of hospitality in the early days of my life.

As a homemaker, Mémé worked hard to keep 42 Academy Road neat, clean, and orderly. She paid attention to details and to the presentation of her home, located in a middle-class neighborhood in the city's west end.

My parents and I stayed there for nine months after I arrived. After we moved out, my mother frequently walked me in the carriage from the city's east side to the west side to visit her mother. When I was about two-years-old, my mother would drop me off at 42 Academy Road for the weekend with my grandparents. The reason given was to get some relief from this very energetic little boy. The weekend ritual continued for approximately six years.

The Academy Road home, with its broad overhanging roof and a reddish-brown earth-stained shingled exterior, provided a warm welcome from the street. The simple, clean, straight-line design of natural materials achieved a visual quality of a sound, solid, and sturdy structure, which spoke to working-class sensibilities. Nature and harmony were valued over the technology of the times.

The Arts and Crafts-style bungalow was plain, comfortable, unimposing, and simple in its outside and inside design. It facilitated a simpler, practical, and efficient way of life while at the same time creating a sense of coziness, beauty, and charm. It cultivated wholesome living as well as peace, comfort, and friendliness.

I felt welcomed at 42 Academy Road. The house was an intimate, open interior space that for me felt like an enclosed refuge, a harbor, an anchor. The dusty rose color of the carpeting was soothing. Bright colored wallpaper patterns of flowers, grasses, lilies, fruits, and vines adorned the walls. These various wallpapers unified the rooms, complimented the architecture, and enhanced the structural effect of the house. The interior woodwork trim was a simplification of the Colonial Revival style. The oak and maple natural hardwood and its trim, simple and quiet in tone added to the feeling of peace, warmth, and comfort. This friendly, pleasant living space welcomed its occupants to share in its simplicity, restfulness, sincerity, and freedom. The French doors, natural light from the many windows, hissing of the steam radiators, beauty of its great fireplace, open staircase, and wainscoting-paneled wooden lining of some of its interior walls, invited its inhabitants to let down, let go, and rest.

The house was a grace given to me through its forms, textures, and colors. In this soulful dwelling place, I felt nurtured, enriched, and inspired by its ability to create a home for my soul and establish a safe, peaceful sanctuary in the world.

The house's tranquility, ease, and calm provided comfort and warmth. I felt like a little Dalai Lama, so respected, reverenced, and appreciated in this paradise.

Mémé watched over and faithfully preserved the soulfulness of the house. Patient, attentive, and filled with care for the residence, she was a dedicated and devoted keeper of the house. She actively directed the affairs of the house. She listened and looked carefully, attending to the small details and particulars of the presentation of the house. In her soft, gentle, quiet style she catered sensitively and unobtrusively to my needs. Usually there was no television, no music, and no real chatting. I felt like I was in a Quaker meeting house with my Mémé. She always gave me permission to be in this quiet environment with my toys.

My Mémé and Pépé's strong presence was always in the background. I can't remember them speaking very much, which added to the quiet, the silence, the stillness, and the peace. Although my grandparents did not display physical affection toward me, I felt their warmth, love, and care. They were pleasant, peaceful, and unhurried human beings. They were both dignified stewards of the home. Humble, self-possessed and hard-working people, their thoughtfulness, generosity, and graciousness made me feel respected, appreciated, and glad to be with them. I always felt safe, secure, relaxed, and able to give myself over to the friendly space of their home.

Here was a soulfulness, a slowed-downness, a richness, and a depth that created joy, delight, contentment, and a contemplative solitude. What made it special was a quiet stillness of mood. It was like a monastery.

This was a sanctuary, a sacred place where I felt truly comfortable. It was a refuge and a retreat that offered an openness, a freshness, a reverence, a resting. I felt protected, anchored, grounded, and securely enclosed. Sitting silently, I sensed a living spirit of the house. The place was filled with goodness. It was a precious place in my life, tangibly and emotionally charged with delight, awe, and joy. A hospitality of heart permeated this home, where I felt accepted, welcomed, warmed, and sustained.

The dining room's large windows received plenty of light from the south and west from eleven in the morning to day's end. Built-in hutches decorated two corners. A large reddish brown, rectangular mahogany table with matching chairs filled the middle of the room. Big table pads always protected the tabletop. They were covered pale white lace tablecloth on top of which rested plate settings complete with cloth napkins and miniature personal salt and pepper shakers. It was like being in a lovely hotel. It was a place of sharing conversation in an atmosphere of love and gratitude. We ate leisurely and were comfortable together in spirit. The room's four windows provided views of the garden outside.

In the solarium, windows gave access to the towering fifty-foot weeping evergreens that acted as borders to the property. The changing seasonal vegetation could also be pleasantly engaged from the same portal. The weather and time of day could be directly observed from the sun parlor. I remember how well the sun lit the room, streaming rays throughout this quiet and meditative room. With windows open in the spring, summer, and fall, you could hear the sounds of crickets, bullfrogs, birds, and the wind whistling through the trees. The windows brought outdoor views and vistas into the house. Birds nested in the Rose of Sharon bushes that surrounded the solarium, and I had a privileged perspective to observe the unfolding of the new generations of robins. The mountain laurel, rhododendrons, azaleas, dogwoods, and the mature apple tree shared their spring flowers. The fragrance of roses, lily of the valley, and lavender transfused the solarium at various times. The solarium also was filled with well cared for houseplants including coleus, ferns, and African violets.

The kitchen was simple, convenient, comfortable, and cheerful with a cozy booth for four built into the north corner of the room. Large windows over the double sink provided views of the backyard trees and shrubs. They also were filled with gorgeous vistas of the sun setting in the west.

The living room was the darkest room in the house because the east-facing windows opened to the closed-in front porch that was surrounded by tall trees. The room featured a fireplace hearth with brickwork that extended from the hearth. On each side of the fireplace was a four-shelf bookcase. Four comfortable stuffed chairs with coffee tables and reading lamps were arranged so that all could view the television in the corner. The natural rich nut-brown tone of the room's woodwork created a mellow, cheery atmosphere. The space was organized into a coherent whole, which delighted the soul. Its order, beauty, and grace invited me to rest and enjoy being myself. The coziness made the space alive, comfortable, and pleasant. Dusty rose carpeting, beige pull-down window shades, tasteful wallpaper in each room added to the quaintness of the interior in this English cottage-like home.

The sacredness of the house was manifested through the everyday architecture of the walls, doors, windows, ornaments, and rooms that connected spirit with matter. The dwelling had beauty, harmony, and radiance. Its pleasant nooks and crannies offered a sense of enclosure. Forty-two

Academy Road was filled with charm and goodness. This sacred space, this holy place, caressed, inspired, and nourished my soul, and continued to renew my spirit. I felt like a pilgrim paying homage to the spirit of this warm, welcoming, cozy, and intimate home. Its depth and simple charm cultivated my well-being and filled me with interior peace and stillness.

Plenty of natural, bright light filled the airy open floor plan and made the house pleasant and cheerful. The aromatic spices of cinnamon and vanilla from Mémé's wonderful cooking of Greek food, especially delicious desserts, excited my senses. The smell of George Washington Great American cherry tobacco from my Pépé's pipe, was an after-dinner evening ritual that awakened me to Pépé's ability to relax as he read his local evening newspaper.

My grandfather, George, was a man of few words, but he was a man with a strong presence. He contributed to the space of 42 Academy Road, which was a powerful place of hospitality for me. I felt he held me in the palms of his firm, strong, and supportive hands and fed me with his warm, gracious smile, and gentle stillness. He secured my space, gave me a place, and protected me.

In this peaceful setting, as a young child I played with the various toys from the toy box. Tinker toys, wooden blocks, a log cabin set, an erector set, and plastic green army men all helped me lose myself in play and imagination. The wool carpet, the beautiful oak and maple handcrafted woodwork, the rays of the sun streaming through the rooms all invited me to enjoy, take delight in the pleasure of experiencing and living in the present moment.

Along with Mémé and Pépé, the house offered me shelter. It received me with care and aliveness. Awe, wonder, and enchantment were gifts it gave me. The whole experience was characterized by depth, stability, and groundedness. The air of simplicity, humility, and coziness permeated the spirit of the house. The dignity and value of good design and caretaking, witness to the sacredness of life as it breathed life into me.

Time at Mémé's was lived in the present; there was no accent on the future or the past. There were no worries. I felt safe and secure. There was no rushing, no hecticness. It was quiet, at times almost verging on silence.

The power of seeing the rays of the sun streaming through the windows stopped me in my tracks. Watching the changing of the seasons, observing the unfolding of the apple tree and the flower and vegetable gardens was calming and guided me to be totally present to the now. The power of the now invited and welcomed me. With it evolved a sense of letting go and surrender and allowed me to experience simply being and experiencing awe, wonder, mystery, and enchantment.

My body was relaxed, at ease, flexible, and grounded. This cultivated a quiet, peaceful, focused way of being that was simply open and receptive to what is, an ease of being there. My body and spirit were invited to rest and be myself. Forty-two Academy Road became a home for my soul that renewed and enlivened wholeness within me. It was a home that still nurtures my soul.

Gratitude continues to well up as I realize how this marker event of hospitality in my life enabled me to experience a solid foundation for my life. A grace was given—and is continually given—as I grow in appreciation for 42 Academy Road where Mémé and Pépé showered me with love, a sense of welcome and hospitality that facilitated my ability to rest and be myself during my earliest years.

Looking back, I had an intimate relationship with this house. I dwelt, abided, stayed with the sacred space of the here and now of this home.

The sacred dimension, the spirit dimension, the infinite, the mystery, the more than, the transcendent, was an unseen face that transformed and nourished me. The dwelling had beauty, wholeness, harmony, and radiance. There was energy that animated me. There was an orderliness that helped me feel secure and in control of my life.

When I pass 42 Academy Road, I sometimes imagine going around its structure with incense, and blessing this holy place. I feel like a pilgrim paying homage to this sacred space that was so good to me, that caressed me, that nourished my heart and soul, and continues to renew my spirit.

In the fall of 1946, Mémé and Pépé graciously welcomed my mother, father, and myself, then a six-month-old unborn child, into their cozy home at 42 Academy Road. Their cottage embraced us for about a year. I continued to experience that embrace nearly every weekend for the next twelve years.

Mémé and Pépé's presence was the second important dimension that contributed to an ongoing experience of hospitality. Always in the background, they were dependent upon God for His care and support, and they were grateful for His Presence in their lives. Mémé and Pépé welcomed me into an atmosphere of love, care, and acceptance. They were patient, kind, and humble. Each in their own way catered to my needs. Their presence was generous, gracious, and filled with goodness. They were peaceful, gentle, simple, unhurried human beings who cultivated my well-being. I was able to learn how to abide, dwell, and be myself.

Nonna

Middle Street in Leominster, Massachusetts, is about a mile long. It begins about a quarter-mile southwest of the city's downtown. Along the street was a coal company and farther down was an oil company, each with large tracts of land. Most of the residential buildings were two- or three-deckers. They were all occupied by families whose last names ended in a vowel, immigrants from Italy who came to America at the turn of the nineteenth century. Many of these Italian-American families were multi-generational and each had four to seven children. From Middle Street, they were able to walk to their jobs in the plastics factories and machine shops.

My Italian grandmother, Victoria, whom we called Nonna, lived at 53 Middle Street. Four blocks from Nonna's house, at the end of Middle Street, was the intersection with Johnson Street, where my mother, father, and I lived on the corner of Johnson and Middle Streets at 52 Johnson Street.

Middle Street was also home to my Great Aunt Mamie, who lived next to the oil company. About 200-feet farther on was Paquette's Garage. There were four houses, and a store at the corner of Middle and 6th Streets. Across the street were a bakery and an undeveloped lot. Five or six houses farther down was our home, the triple-decker apartment building called "the block" that housed six families. We lived in the second-floor apartment on the left side; my Aunt Sunny and her husband, Wilfred, lived on the right side. I remember so well Uncle Wilfred knocking on our door about 8:00 a.m. almost every morning, asking me to come over for breakfast with him and Aunt Sunny. He had just gotten home from his 11:00 to 7:00 shift as a police officer with the Leominster Police Department. At the time, they had no children. I was it.

By age three, I would walk across the porch to visit with Aunt Sunny and/or Uncle Wilfred. Aunt Sunny would tell me stories about her family and read books to me. Uncle Wilfred would bring me over to help tend to the horse, pig, chickens, sheep, and goats in his barn across the street.

Cooking was one of my aunt's favorite pastimes. I would run over to her apartment many times a day. She would yell my name, "Vincent!" with excitement. "Come in. I haven't seen you for a while!" I remember feeling her warmth, care, affection, and joy that I was visiting once again. She made me feel truly special and at-home in her apartment, where I would play with my toys in her kitchen and parlor.

A quarter of a mile from the apartment was our Roman Catholic parish St. Anna's Church, which had been founded for Italian immigrants. I remember the bells ringing for the hours of the Angelus, at 6:00 a.m., noon, and 6:00 p.m. each day.

On Sundays, the church bells rang five minutes before the start of each Mass. The bells rang as a casket was carried out of the church at the end of a funeral. The bells pealed at the end of a wedding ceremony as the newly married couple emerged from the church to walk down the long flight of stairs.

When I was seven, my father suggested that I become an altar boy. From then until I was twelve, I would walk from the church after serving Mass or from downtown to Nonna's house and followed the same ritual each time. I would gently knock on the back door and would hear her warm greeting: "Come in!" I would open the door and there my Nonna would be sitting, having her coffee, cooking, cleaning, and/or crocheting. She would immediately say, "Come sit down and I will make the coffee."

Although Nonna did not display affection by hugging me, she would expect me to hug and kiss her. She was the queen of the family and would look forward to visits from family members.

Her small kitchen offered welcoming comfort. As you walked directly into the kitchen from the outside back door, there was a yellow, oval table with chrome edging, chrome legs, and four matching comfortable chairs. There also were two more matching yellow chairs, a wooden rocking chair, a gas stove, a refrigerator, a double sink with counters on each side. Above the counters were cabinets that stored dishes and food. The kitchen table was used for dining as well as her workspace for making Italian cookies and macaroni.

Whether it was eighty degrees or two degrees outside, she would make the coffee. If this was coffee between meals, she would ask me to put a few Italian cookies on a plate to enjoy with our coffee. If it was around mealtime, she would ask me to set the table for the meal, cut the paper napkins in half and give each diner half a napkin, a continuation of a Depression-era ritual.

Once arranging for coffee or a meal was completed, we could now sit down to enjoy each other's company, eating while sharing stories about her garden, her shopping deals, her cooking, and her childhood in a small village outside the city of Rome, in Italy.

Nonna's garden was very much part of her home and her life. She had flower gardens and a vegetable garden. Every year she would plant many gardens on her property, faithfully water them at 6:30 a.m. and 6:30 p.m.

My grandmother would graciously invite me into her beautiful gardens and teach me the fundamentals of gardening and beautification of the land. She had a sacred connection with her plot of land, and she passed that reverence and respect on to me.

I found myself very much at home both inside and outside Nonna's home. She cultivated a space and time just to be present to what was before her and around her. Her welcoming presence beckoned me to sit, relax, and enjoy myself around her table, in her gardens, and to listen to her stories.

Nonna's neighborhood was home to the cathedral-sized Gothic church, St. Cecilia's, which dominated the skyline. Her house, a quarter-mile away, was in the shadow of the church's magnificent grand steeple. The bell tower spired into the sky and the carillon would ring out sacred songs and also rang for the Angelus. The carillon rang on the hour until the final ringing out of the Angelus. They rang on days of weddings and funerals as well.

Aunts, uncles, cousins, great aunts, and a great uncle all lived on Middle Street, which was lined with maples and Dutch elm trees that shaded the street in summer. In the spaces between the trees, you could see the beautiful spires of St. Cecilia's Church and you could hear the ringing of its bells throughout the day. These relatives were all members of working-class families and most worked in the local plastics factories. Their homes were kept neat and clean and most had both flower and vegetable gardens.

Nonna's garden included two mature pear trees, each at least fifty feet tall. One bore Bartlett pears, the other Anjou. She also had a large cherry tree, an apple tree, and a magnificent Dutch Elm tree that was at least seventy-five feet tall. In the spring, the pink and white blossoms filled the garden with beauty and the aroma of the season. There always seemed to be a gentle breeze that rustled the leaves and added to the freshness of the air throughout the spring, summer and fall. There were many lilac bushes that added to the mix of fragrances in the yard, which also included the smell of freshly watered gardens and grass, purple, pink, blue, and white hydrangeas. Throughout the garden, forsythia bloomed in the spring.

The back of my Nonna's property bordered land owned by a railroad. There was a section of dense trees and brush and then a ninety-foot bank of sand and gravel. At the top of that hill was the railroad loading depot. Sometimes the hobos—migratory workers and homeless people—who road in railroad cars found their way down to the woods next to Nonna's land. When my cousin and I cut through the woods and the sandbank to the depot station, we occasionally bumped into a man or groups of men sleeping in the woods. Scared, we quickly ran away.

My Aunt Mamie, who was divorced, lived with her two high-school age daughters in a home on one side of Nonna's house. Mamie, who worked in a factory during the day, was always welcoming to me. The people living on the other side of Nonna's house were more recent Italian immigrants who only spoke Italian. We did not get to know them. Across the street from

Nonna, more friends and relatives lived in triple-deckers with open space for gardens of their own.

Family offered a strong sense of safety, security, identity, and protection from the outside world. Providing a stable, consistent, constant, cohesive, and well-ordered existence, the family remained a sanctuary, a world closely knit together with a unified philosophy. The family emphasized mutual giving and taking. In our family, you knew where you stood; there was no ambivalence.

Drenched in a culture, you also acquire roots, traditions, customs, rituals, beliefs, and meanings.

Home ownership was a symbol of family, not status. At the center of the home was the kitchen. The table was the center of the kitchen and food was far more than eating. It was a ritual of being-with, a religious ceremony, a work of art, and an event. Pleasure came from eating and sharing food with others. This was central to daily life. Food was considered a private source of emotional and physical solace. Around the table, people talked to each other, shared joy and sorrow, victories, and disappointments, the past and the future, hopes and dreams. Food represented home and it was around the table of food that you shared your spirit with each other. Eating around the table was a relaxed, leisurely, warm, supportive, and comfortable atmosphere in which people were able to simply be themselves with one another.

Everyone was welcomed into the home. People were greeted with respect, excitement, and care. You would hear people say, "Sit down at the table and have a sandwich." Around the table people would share their stories and simply be with each other. They developed the ability to experience intense enjoyment of home life, savoring in a leisurely manner the present moment with family and friends.

I vividly recall the ritual of sitting in Nonna's backyard. My relatives would form a circle with their lawn chairs and would begin to speak about and to listen to each other's joys and difficulties of the day. Inevitably, as the darkness of evening fell upon the gathering, my relatives participated in the ritual of coffee and Italian cookies and then continued the conversation, philosophizing about how to deal with all that was discussed that day.

My Nonna provided space and time just to be present and enjoy what was before me. She offered me a strong sense of safety, security, and identity. She was a sanctuary to me. The experience was a relaxed, leisurely, warm, supportive, and comfortable one in which we were both able to simply be ourselves with one another with respect, excitement, and care. I came to know this as hospitality.

The Hospitality of Julie Country Day School

When I was seven, we moved to the city's west side and into our new ranch-style house on an unpaved road and surrounded by woods.

There were four anchor points to nature for me from age seven to eighteen. About a half-mile from our house began a forest that went for miles and miles, up and over the hills in what seemed like mountains to me. Hiking through the forest periodically, my friends and I would walk into clearings that were old farmlands.

A quarter-mile from my house there was a twenty-eight-acre pond with its own dam. The pond was fed by a brook and many springs. During my childhood years, I was able to explore the pond from the perspective of a canoe, a rowboat, and a motorboat as well as through waterskiing, swimming, and playing hockey.

There was a finger-shaped island that created coves. There were pine groves on the island, which was connected by a bridge to the shore. I often would go lie down on a bed of pine needles, look at the sky, and listen to the sound of the wind blowing through the pine groves. Eventually, I identified that sound as the sound of God.

We did a lot of fishing in the pond, which also was home to snapping turtles, regular turtles, frogs, eels, algae, water lilies, water grasses, muskrats, beavers, swans, geese, ducks, and herons. Most of the time the water was crystal clear.

Another quarter-mile from my house was Julie Country Day School, operated by the Sisters of Notre Dame. The history of the land and the development of the property has long fascinated me.

The nuns lived on a thirty-acre tract of land that dates back to Joel Crosby, who served during the Revolutionary War as General George

Washington's bodyguard. After the war, Crosby bought land in Leominster and became a gentleman farmer, growing peaches, pears, plums, nectarines, apples, grapes, and berries. Later, the farm was operated by the Miles family.

In 1908, industrialist and president of the Fitchburg Railway Company Harry L. Pierce bought the seventeen-acre property and built a twenty-nine-room eclectic mansion that was called Grayling Hall. He wanted his Southern belle bride to feel at home in this small New England city and to be happy as he built his financial empire of railroads and tract housing.

Grayling Hall sat on a hill overlooking Monoosnoc Hill, home to a granite quarry. The estate included a palm conservatory, a horse stable, and an extensive horse paddock. The grounds featured an English-style landscape with sweeping vistas across rolling lawns, distant groves of trees, natural ponds, and grottos. This botanical garden was situated at an altitude of 1,000 feet. Completing the vista from the hillside setting, Pierce had Monoosnoc Brook dammed to create the nearby twenty-eight-acre body of water that became known as Pierce Pond.

Pierce had commissioned a place of peace, solace and inspiration that was filled with the mystery of creation. The manor, surrounded by the grandness of the English-style landscaping, a cultivated space, was an artistic expression inviting contemplation, calm, stillness, and serenity.

In 1914, Frank S. Ewing, proprietor of the Minute Tapioca Company, purchased Grayling Hall from Evlenia L. Thayer. Known as "King Tapioca," Ewing was the president of Minute Tapioca, the company that invented tapioca. He bought the estate for his wife, a former ballet dancer. In 1930, devastated by her sudden death, Ewing sold the estate to the Sisters of Notre Dame. A neighbor, Bernard Doyle, eventually donated his nearby thirteen-acre property to the nuns.

The enormous three-story twenty-nine-room Neo-Flemish Grayling Hall became their convent. Outside you could feel the beauty and pleasure of nature all around you. There were acres and acres of paths of rhododendrons, azaleas, and mountain laurel. Acres of meticulously manicured lawns surrounded both the convent and the school. The back of the convent had a lovely terrace overlooking the pond Harry Pierce had had built at the foot of the hill upon which the mansion stood.

In 1941, the Sisters of Notre Dame opened a one-room school in the former horse stables. During the '40s and '50s, they gradually established a grammar school providing classes from kindergarten through grade eight in the converted stables. The thirty-acre property was surrounded by 166 acres of woodland, scenic meadows, and several historic filled-in cellar holes. The whole area was and remains a sanctuary of abundant flora and fauna.

There was a forest of red maple swamp, a small scrub swamp, wet meadows, and an intermittent pool. The forest was supported by the slow decomposition of leaf litter. A white pine forest, red pine oak, and mixed hard wood trees populated the woodlands.

Throughout the property were relatively large and contiguous areas of open grassland habitats. Old stone walls acted as fences marking old historic field boundaries.

Large tracts of natural, undeveloped land formed the 4,265-acre Leominster State Forest on the city's western border. This whole area was populated by lemmings, muskrats, coyotes, wolves, red and grey foxes, black bears, raccoons, weasels, ermine, mink, deer, wild turkeys, Canada geese, opossums, moles, bats, hares, rabbits, chipmunks, woodchucks, squirrels, beavers, and field mice.

Discovering a Magical Connection to Nature

On this property, there was an overgrown entrance that I discovered when I was seven years old. It all seemed magical to me. Once I fought my way through the entrance, there was a quarter-mile path outlined or bordered by rhododendrons, azaleas, mountain laurel, and various blossoming trees, such as dogwood, tulip trees, magnolias, and chestnut trees.

Along my walk to Julie Country Day School, was a charming little cottage where Mrs. Dillon lived. She had a housekeeper/companion named Ruthie, who hired and trained me at age eight as their gardener. She was lovely, kind, and understanding of the limits of my age. Her training helped me understand the fundamentals of cultivating flowers as I developed a deep appreciation of landscaping. In winter, I shoveled their property and brought wood into the house for their fireplace. Supportive of me, Ruthie often spoke to me about my future.

As I grew older, I became part of the landscape crew tending to Julie Country Day School. By the time I was ten, I recruited kids from my neighborhood to volunteer to cultivate these gardens. The payoff from the nuns was a sugary drink we kids called bug juice and cookies with an occasional candy bar thrown in.

The opportunity to experience and engage with the intriguing space that was Julie Country Day School has been a most enduring reward. I recall a break in the privet shrubbery at the entrance where I experienced an invitation to walk through the six-foot wide space between the pillars onto the strolling path umbrellaed by rows of cedars, hemlocks, weeping spruce, and evergreens that formed a cave-like feature. I moved from the public street of Lindell Avenue over a six-foot stretch of grass through the pillared gateway and then traveled across eight more feet of green grass into a cavern formed by two rows of evergreens supported by the undergrowth of rhododendrons, laurel, and winterberries.

Along the path, there was a noticeable change of light, sound, surface, level, and direction. I transitioned through the natural enclosure. From the pillars through the *allée* of evergreens and shrubs, there was a darker, quieter, stiller atmosphere. It smelled fresh from the build-up of evergreen needles on the ground. It was naturally softer, a cushion on the earth. The build-up of the plant material absorbed the sound. Yet, as the breeze or sometimes the wind blew through the *allées*, it created a harmony of the sound of silence. The length of this grove of evergreens was not very long, maybe seventy-five feet. But within this space, I continued to experience very powerful moments of being connected to the earth, to the beauty of nature.

In going through the pillars into the *allée* of the grove of evergreens and shrubs, I experienced the beginning of the path as entering a sanctuary, an interior site. This first fifty yards of the path was a transitional movement from public to private, outer to inner, exterior to interior, profane to the sacred. During the spring, it was mesmerizing. In the grassy knolls, there were daffodils, crocuses, mayflowers, and the very structured English-style flower gardens. My senses became more alive, more comfortable, and at ease.

Journeying through the pillars I felt like I was coming home. The beginning of walking the path awakened a feeling of being at home and I was filled with a sense of peace. The sacred site could only be approached by foot and was gradually disclosed and revealed one step, one threshold, at a time. The combination of the gateway of the pillars and the umbrella of the *allée* of the grove of evergreens created a sensation of approaching mystery.

Over the years, the property at 401 Lindell Avenue in Leominster has held an irresistible attractiveness for me. In addition to my one-to-one interaction with the nuns, my consciousness was massaged by the property upon which the convent and school rested.

There was a power, an allure, a captivation that the property and land had over me. The best way I can put it is that in stepping onto the property I was filled with a sense of the sacred. I felt welcomed by the grandeur of the English-style landscaping. It was intentionally and deliberately orchestrated that way. And it seemed that if you were open with your heart to the command of the land and its buildings, you would be offered a new gift of awe and wonder each day.

These gifts were seasonal. They could be fresh footprints of local fauna in new fallen snow, the unfolding of the buds on the tulip trees and carpets of mayflowers in spring, the coolness of the shade of various groves of trees thanks to the filled-out summer foliage, and magnificent changing colors of leaves in the fall.

Somewhere deep inside of me I felt welcomed by the land and its property. And although I was a young boy, I felt connected and at one with the beauty of nature, its colors, textures, shapes, and sizes. The pleasure I received opened up in me a sense of awe and wonder. I had this park in my immediate neighborhood and I was immersed in its magnificence day in and day out for six years of my life.

During each of the four seasons of the year, it continued to share its unfolding presence and I found myself touched deeply in my soul by what was offered to me. Changes in the weather seemed to provide a different place each day. The property called my mind, heart, and soul to what the nuns had quoted their foundress as saying: "The good God is so very good today."

My Julie Country Day schoolmates and I would sing a song at school, repeating over and over again the words, "The good God is so very good today." Etched into my mind and heart, the song expressed appreciation and gratitude for me. I was enchanted by the property. It drew me in, engaged me, beckoned me, delighted me, and captivated me. On many occasions, I was simply overjoyed by how the property spoke to me a sense of welcome and invitation to make myself at home.

For me, the property had a sense of liveliness that gave rise to a sense of excitement, delight, and pure enjoyment. It was simply very pleasurable to walk on this property. It seemed to be a home away from home. At times, I was enthralled and enraptured by my experience of the property. It awakened, stirred up an aesthetic admiration for the beauty around me. I was indeed moved deeply by the goodness of God, who created all of this in this park. Not knowing how I was being formed and shaped by the nuns, I can see now that they helped me make connections with cloud formations, weather, beauty, the land, and the goodness of God and His creation.

The Sisters made me feel very welcome. They treated me with loving kindness and were openly appreciative of the work I was doing. They often conversed with me after school as I walked with them across the street, carrying their briefcases. My role grew from cleaning one room to receiving a key to the school in the fifth grade, so I could come and go as needed to attend to my expanding role as junior custodian/groundskeeper.

Over the years this property has been used as a college preparatory boarding school for boys, a rest home for nuns stricken with tuberculosis, a house of formation for the Sisters of Notre Dame, called *"Villa Immaculata."* The Sisters opened Julie Country Day School in the former the horse stable in 1941, and gradually added to the school facility. They sold Grayling Hall to the Trustees of Reservations in 1999. In 2001, the Trustees opened ten-acre Pierce Park that is now part of the 170-acre Doyle Center and Community Park.

For this ten-year-old boy, the property was a glorious respite from my life at home, which was chaotic. Remember the definition of hospitality as welcome, make yourself at home in order to rest and be yourself. The deeper sense of rest is to be, abide, and dwell. This kind of psychological rest—soothing to the soul, allowing me to hold the world lightly, and be at peace—was the tremendous gift this cathedral of nature conferred upon me.

The Human Experience of Hospitality

These personal descriptions of hospitality bound together illuminate an aspect of human experience. The pattern that is disclosed is that hospitality is a disposition, a particular way or manner of being. It is a distinctive frame of mind, an approach, a stance toward life.

Hospitality as a disposition is a particular way of being that welcomes another and invites the other to make themselves at home in order to rest and be themselves.

In this chapter, we have presented three descriptions of the human experience of hospitality. Having reflected on the narratives of Mémé and Pépé, Nonna, and Julie Country Day as phenomena of hospitality in a rigorous, systematic, and disciplined manner, our searching has disclosed an essential structure of hospitality.

Our understanding of hospitality has been revealed as a process in which the other is welcomed and invited to make himself at home in order that he may rest and be himself.

In the following chapters, we will make explicit what is implicit, make visible what is invisible about the phenomenon of hospitality. Welcome, make yourself at home in order to rest and be yourself will be our focus. Shedding light on what this means will be our goal.

– 3 –
Cultural Analysis

Hospitality in the American tradition is our focus. The context and the setting is American culture. The purpose of this chapter is to describe and articulate how the American culture has all too often today has become an obstacle to the unfolding of the experience of hospitality in our everyday lives. I will continue to use the method of being rigorous, systematic, and disciplined to understand the lived experience of the phenomenon of hospitality in a thoughtful and helpful way. This manner of reflection will help illuminate the rich meaning, intention, and significance of the human experience of hospitality.

Sooner or later, we discover that we have been born into a pre-existing world, ready-made with all sorts of stipulations that powerfully mold us to their ways and means of living. We call this ready-made world "culture."

Culture is an orientation that shows us how to live as human beings in the world. It provides explanations about the world, a comprehensive set of directions about what to do, how to do it, and how to feel about what we do. These directives are the cherished legacy passed on by ancestors; this ancestral legacy is packaged in customs and traditions.

Customs and traditions are institutionalized patterns that cover every aspect of life. They teach us fundamental beliefs, moral and ethical laws, and practical tips for living. They define certain tastes and certify dress codes, personal hygiene, work, and play. These directives set rituals of worship, social life, art, music, literature, and celebrations.

All this describes a socialization process. Socialization starts with parents and family and expands to include community, state, region, and nation. Culture happens in our homes, neighborhoods, and communities; it takes place in our churches, parks, schools, and workplaces. Through socialization, we are schooled in the culture.

The culture fits our eyes with a certain lens, tunes our ears to certain frequencies, and adjusts our hearts to the rhythm set by our communities. As a result, culture selects certain values, attitudes, dispositions, rules, behaviors, and habits. We live within clearly prescribed parameters. Children soak up what the culture offers. They grow up as part of the culture and become representatives of the cultural standard.

Within the larger framework of culture, particular ethnic, religious, gender, political, economic, artistic, literary, and occupational subcultures exist with their own traditions.

Cultural Traditions

Some cultural traditions may completely undermine a healthy body, mind, and spirit — the foundational dimensions of human living. There are functional traditions, which focus on individual performance and achievement and foster unfettered greed and profit. They encourage preoccupation with power, wealth, and status.

Such traditions seek to attain perfection and mastery of the world—and others—through the intellect. They feed an inflated ego that demands immediate attention and gratification. This kind of ego manipulates the world to conform to its wishes or suffer its vicious rage. Autarchic traditions espouse a rugged individualism of excessive dependence upon oneself. They cultivate dispositions of invulnerability and non-empathy. A self-centered belief in taking care of number one prevails. Finally, the traditions of market individualism foster unlimited liberty to engage in business in any way possible to increase profits. This tradition makes money a god and promotes dispositions of "me first."

On the other hand, there are faith traditions and family or communal traditions that nurture dispositions of care, compassion, generosity, kindness, empathy, community, sharing, and service to others. Such traditions help take us out of self-occupation and excessive self-interest. They draw us into intimate and empathic relationships with others in the world. These traditions are nourished and maintained through an attunement with spirit that opens us into a relationship with the sacred. This can happen directly or through beliefs associated with the worship of a transcendent being who created and cares for us. These traditions place meaning and purpose in a larger context than just that of material fulfillment.

However, authoritarian rule, rigid dogmatism, and strict adherence to orthodoxy can undermine these dispositions. Such strictures can stifle the spirit, discipline, and discount the body, and lobotomize the mind through detailed and strict ethical commandments and rules. Thus, the very opportunity to take us out of ourselves and temper our inflated egos turns back on itself and fails to achieve its original purpose.

We are focusing on the experience of hospitality in American culture. Our questions are many, but I firmly believe that if we continue to be rigorous, systematic, and disciplined, we will be able to address these questions in a thoughtful and helpful way.

At any moment in my life, I have been influenced by others who have gone before me in my family, neighborhood, town, state, and country. The Western civilization into which I was born and the events of history during my lifetime leave their traces in my being. Everything I experience contributes to the process of my becoming and my development of self.

The American Dream

Early American life focused on the functional dimension of being human. Attention was singularly centered on hard work and duty. The American Dream inspired the pursuit of the good life, trying to make it in the world, and take one's place at the table. The goal was to obtain happiness by enjoying life, liberty, health, and safety. Life was to be better, richer, and fuller. Capitalism as the moral socio-political system freed people to act in their rational self-interest—that is, to do whatever one wanted. Material success only reinforced the belief that Americans could overcome any obstacle to achieve, progress, and accomplish their dream. It was up to the individual to make it happen.

Our capitalistic economic consumer system promised upward mobility. Profit seeking, competition, buying, and selling became a major vein pulsing through American culture. Losing, winning, measuring up took on a primary focus in living. The process of acquiring, possessing, and accumulating goods and services drove the economy and individuals. Merit, talent, and status were all part of the American language.

Becoming rich, famous and/or powerful became the ideal. Biggest, best, fullest, richest filled the headlines that guided people's energy, discipline, and perseverance, bolstering productivity and responsibility. With all these cultural values in place, our American Dream became a reality for many. Growth, expansion, and development increased.

Functional and Spiritual Cultural Dimensions

The culture into which we are born has a formative and fundamental impact on us all. Culture is like the air we breathe. As we reflect on the culture, we see that the functional affects all aspects of everyday living.

The culture and its values in today's world may render the human body an instrument of the rational, egoic, technologically focused mind. The body becomes a product that must be packaged to be appealing, attractive, and sexy. Our bodies become poster boards of picture-perfect things while their primordial aliveness is hidden. At the same time, we commit to a rescue mission of rehabilitation, pumping up our bodies with whatever is new and improved, whatever will make us "the best."

The functional dimension overwhelms the spirit dimension of who we are. Not anchored in our bodies, the functional has its way with us. It anesthetizes our spirit. Awe and wonder are displaced in our everyday lives. In pushing, rushing, and speeding, we no longer see, hear, smell, taste, or touch the depths that everyday life offers. The mystery, the depth and breadth of all that remains dormant, sealed off, and covered over. The sacred dimension of life is displaced. The moon, the stars, nature, and the miracle of the human body no longer speak to us. We are no longer amazed, surprised, or excited. Everything has its place, its function to keep us alive, breathing, and getting by without appreciation and gratitude for what is, for what exists, from the perspective of the spirit.

The Impact of American Culture

Culture has a powerful impact on our lives. It can open or close off the depth and richness that life has to offer. We need to develop a relaxed and attentive presence to hold the gift of the everyday lightly, kindly, tenderly, and compassionately. When we do that, our bodies become more awake, aware, and attentive to what is. Open and receptive, our eyes and ears see and hear the powerful drama that is before us. Our hearts are touched by the here and now, and we are invited to rest in the hands of the Mystery.

My premise is that American culture too often has become a problem in relationship to the living out of the human experience of hospitality in our everyday lives. How could it be a problem? This is what I am raising for inquiry and consideration. How is the culture a problem? In what way or manner has it become an obstacle to the unfolding of hospitality as a human disposition?

This all brings me back to my original question: What does it mean to be human? What does it mean to be human in the American culture? From the perspective of the American culture, I hope to find an answer to our problem. I will posit that the American culture *is* the problem. By dwelling with the question what does it mean to be human in the American culture, I hope to shed light on an answer.

The answer to the question resides in our bodies. Listening to the still, quiet voice of our bodies, we will uncover and reveal the answer. The disposition of hospitality can be easily covered over because we are immersed in American culture. It is so close to us that we cannot hear, see, or sense it. Our bodies have been anesthetized.

The American culture is not just an intellectual concept. It is concrete. It has a history. There is a story to be told and reflected upon. What happened to the phenomenon of hospitality in this culture?

The toxins of American culture seep into our bodies and we are rendered numb, devoid of sensation. This insensibility renders us paralyzed. We cannot feel. We become indifferent to how we are being dragged by the flow of American culture.

As we get out of bed in the morning, it is like we pinch our noses and leap into the rushing, tumultuous flow of American culture. Our hope is that eventually we will be brought back to our bed in the evening. It may be difficult to get to sleep or to sleep without interruption. We may be suffering with anxiety and/or depression. Thoughts of the morning may intrude. Worry over returning to the tumult may rob us of sleep.

As a way of anchoring the narrative about culture and its meaning, we refer to the Introduction. There I shared my experience of hospitality as a child. The image I am retrieving is that of sitting at the kitchen table of my Italian grandmother, Nonna, in the city of Leominster, Massachusetts.

The plastic comb-making industry began in Leominster and went on to play a major role in the birth of the plastics industry. Leominster became known as the Plastics Pioneer City and the plastics industry provided the foundation of the city's economy for years.

Leominster was a white, blue-collar working-class community with several ethnic enclaves, namely Italian-American, French-Canadian, Irish, and Jewish. Each ethnic group had its own social clubs, such as the Franco-American Social Hall, the Colombo Hall, where members gathered to play cards, socialize, and eat and drink.

At the end of World War II, the economy started to expand as members of the armed forces returned home. The American focus on progress, hard work, persistence, and endurance helped drive economic development in Leominster.

Within its small-town atmosphere, through its ethnic neighborhoods and communities, the people of Leominster lived out values, customs, and traditions that emphasized loyalty, honor, and human dignity. Living simple lives with a sense of duty to family and work characterized everyday life. Resilience, adaptability, and self-preservation were fostered. The simple pleasures of food and drink were important aspects of the local culture.

A strong emphasis was placed on success. The city of Leominster embraced the American Dream of getting ahead by achieving success. Attitude, determination, and desire comprised the formula for success: live in the present and grab the brass ring.

When my grandfather arrived from Greece in 1912 and my other grandfather arrived from Italy in 1914, they were both seeking the American Dream. My Greek grandfather eventually opened The Boston Confectionery Store, which became a thriving business and a Leominster tradition for more than forty years. My Italian grandfather became a successful foreman in one of the larger plastic factories.

Leominster in the late '40s became part of the post-WWII economic boom. GIs returned home with a sense of unity from fighting together. They had had a common purpose of fighting the war and now, back home in Leominster, they had a common purpose of financially surviving, deepening their sense of security and identity. They were Americans and they wanted to live out the American Dream.

Opportunity was knocking and they came to value certain things. Family came first. Communal respect and solidarity with others were the American way. Becoming financially successful, getting ahead, and being in position to buy a house was part of achieving the dream.

A lot was going on inside and outside themselves. The complexities of human experience became a challenge as they grew older together while building a postwar community. Although not a highly educated group of people, these mainly white, blue-collar working-class men and women all contributed to the community's underlying cultural story of what it meant to be a human being.

I was born into a ready-made world orientation. This culture directed and informed my everyday life. It acted as a background to my life as a child. It implicitly pervaded, supported, and bound my life together. Through its values, customs, and practices, this culture provided coherence and continuity in my life. The people ahead of me continued to carve the path that I was to follow. It was part of the deal of life. It was how the reality of my life was socially constructed.

Values, morals, and ethical beliefs of the community were lived out through shared social practices, symbols, customs, habits, rituals, and traditions. As a way of concretizing this, let us look back at my city, Leominster, and focus on how religion, politics, education, and ethnic customs, values, and traditions massaged people's thinking and perception about the meaning of life. What was life all about? Various institutions provided answers to these questions in a soulful manner. They continued to support the city's people and implicitly what it meant to be human and humane to each other.

In the middle of downtown Leominster is a section in Memorial Square called The Common. There the Civil War Monument stands. The names of major battles and hometown soldiers who died are inscribed on the monument. Other monuments have been erected on Memorial Square. As people pass the beautifully arranged oasis of gardens, they are called to remember some of the city's history and culture. These identifying headstones are markers, symbols of independence, personal achievement, community success, self-sufficiency, and equality. All these characteristics of Leominster dance around in Memorial Square, quietly witnessing significant aspects of the city's culture.

Memorial Square is a witness to soulfulness. Our ancestors gave their lives to keep us free. Each day these cultural symbols continue to honor with dignity the sacred meaning of our heroic war dead of the Civil War, World War I, World War II, the Korean War, and the Vietnam War. These beloved men and women sacrificed their lives so we could live ours. They are witness and testimony to the connective tissue that weaves, binds, and joins its citizens.

Another strong, long-time, and proud dimension of the culture is competitive team sports. The historic football rivalry between Leominster and Fitchburg begins with a 10:00 a.m. kickoff on Thanksgiving Day. This rivalry, which began in 1894, is known to be one of the oldest high school football rivalries in the country.

American Little League and Babe Ruth League baseball have helped generations of kids learn to play on a team, demonstrate good sportsmanship, build friendships, and develop leadership skills. As Boy Scouts and Girl Scouts, children also embraced core values of being trustworthy, loyal, helpful, friendly, courteous, kind, obedient, cheerful, thrifty, brave, clean, and reverent. Scouts were trained in the responsibilities of participation-citizenship, honesty, integrity, moral values, and character and leadership building.

Other shared social practices, symbols, customs, habits, rituals, and traditions that formed and shaped the culture of Leominster were its ten churches and congregations, the Parks and Recreation Department, Leominster Hospital School of Nursing, Leominster Public Library, and the three local movie theaters. Whalom Park, with its traditional English-style gardens and walking paths, its ballroom, roller skating arena, amusement park with roller coaster, merry-go-round, Ferris wheel, and a large lake for swimming, boating, and picnicking was enjoyed by all.

The Girl Scouts' Drum and Bugle Corps, brass marching band, synchronized marching team, Colonial Band, military band, and the Kingsmen Drum and Bugle Corps all participated in the Memorial Day, the Fourth of July, and the Johnny Appleseed parades. City Hall was also a social and cultural center that featured fashion shows, fine plays, comic operas, elegant balls, junior and senior proms, and weekly rock and roll dancing events. Churches and other civic and social organizations sponsored chicken barbecues, spaghetti dinners, ham and bean suppers, and pancake breakfasts.

Along streets lined with stately elms and maples, Italian bakeries pumped out delicious bread and pastries. There was a store that sold fish brought in from the docks of Boston every day. Foster Grant and Dupont continued to supply the United States with toothbrushes, combs, sunglasses, and hairpieces. The G.A. Gane shirt factory, which was the world's largest manufacturer of men's white dress shirts, was another company that contributed to Leominster's cultural unfolding.

Over the years, Leominster's cultural threads laced and intertwined its people. Its culture gave its people spirit, encouragement, support, and a liveliness to grow older together bearing witness to each other as they sang their songs, danced their dances, and played their instruments. The cultural life force seemed to stream through each of us as time unfolded: births and deaths were witnessed; little children were brought to school for the first time; and high school and college graduations were celebrated.

The hospital was there to heal us. The police and fire departments were there to protect us. Grocery stores were there to feed us. The sewer, water, and health departments were there to keep us healthy and whole.

The highway department cared for our roads and streets. All these aspects of our community were part of the culture that vitally and functionally anchored and animated our way of being as a city.

Egoism as a Virtue

Continuing to answer the question about culture and what it means, there is one last thread—the egoic, more specifically, narcissism. Culture has to do with the egoic and with the human spirit. The cultural dimension of the functional covers over the human spirit and reduces hospitality to a doing, a performing, a functioning. The human spirit dimension of hospitality becomes numbed, anesthetized, and frozen. What follows is an articulation of the cultural dimension of the egoic aspect of human experience as an obstacle to the unfolding of hospitality as emerging from the human spirit.

A major influence on the unfolding of the American culture in the '40s through the '50s was the writer Ayn Rand. What does it mean to be human from the perspective of Ayn Rand, who became an important American cultural figure? In her worldview, the moral purpose of one's life is the pursuit of one's own happiness and comfort. This author and philosopher of two best-selling novels (*The Fountainhead*[8], *Atlas Shrugged*[9]), believed that greed is good, and that egoism is a virtue of selfishness.[10]

As a teacher and director of people's unfolding lives, she came to value reason above any other human value. Reason was the only absolute value. She believed that our happiness is the moral purpose of our lives. Productive achievement is our noblest activity. She expounded a morality of rational self-interest. Rational and ethical egoism should be what continues to shape and form our everyday ways of living our lives, she espoused. She strongly rejected altruism. Her focus was on self, the ego, not the regard for or devotion to the welfare of others.

The virtue of selfishness is cultivated by having a good sense of self-esteem.

---

8 The Fountainhead
9 Atlas Shrugged
10 See, for example, The Virtue of Selfishness.

This means you are confident of your efficacy and worth and have a basic conviction that you are competent to live your life as you please.

Ayn Rand and her student/partner, Nathaniel Branden, created a cultural ethic that centered on the self. By self, they meant: me, myself, and I. I am "it." It's all up to me. One needs to esteem oneself as the maker, producer, the designer of one's life. They believed that the self should always be the central concern and value in our lives. We should be living to realize our own selves for our own good. Thus, we are called to self-centeredness. We need to worship the self as our god, as the all-powerful self can be anything that it wants to be.

The ideology of the self, the ethic of self-esteem and self-expression reinforce the posture of being all about self. From this perspective, we need to be committed to being self-sufficient, self-determined, self-made, self-reliant as well as self-centered, self-absorbed, and self-preoccupied. In being all about self, we become self-fulfilled, self-actualized, and self-important.

By being fixated on being right, successful, and recognized by competing, outdoing, and winning, the self becomes very efficient and effective at living an ideology of individualism. The doctrine of individualism emphasizes that the interests of the individual are—or ought to be—ethically paramount. That is, the conception of all values, rights, and duties originates in individuals.

Pragmatism assists the self in achieving the goal of "the sky is the limit." Striving, asserting, pushing, and straining are traits of pragmatism. There is an emphasis on focusing on what works to get the job done, to immediately, quickly, instantly, complete the task in the short run. Pragmatism is action, making, producing, and completing. Power, control, mastery, and domination are the goals. Fame and fortune are celebrated in the victory dance of the self being raised up as the winner, the bearer of the crown that proclaims: "I have the right to it all and have it now as I travel in the fast lane." Engine revved up, speeding out of the box with a busy mind trapped in its own thinking, lost in the materialist consumer society that spends billions of dollars to get into my mind to convince me that, if I only buy this or that, I will for one more day be king or queen of the day.

Rand believed that a functioning society would be the result if every person focused on himself or herself. We should not be other-oriented. Rather, we should be focused on our own self-interest. She stated that the "I" does not have responsibility or obligation to the other. From her perspective, the "common good" is nonsense. Life should always be focused on me, myself, and I. The good life is the ability of each of us to pursue our own happiness and comfort.

This is achieved by following the Gospel of Prosperity, which is based on a sacred commitment to follow the profit motive through self-made performance, personal achievement, and obtaining material success. We always need to keep our eye on the prize, that is, the glorification of our personal happiness by practicing the moral virtue of the primacy of self-interest and embracing the belief that greed is good and that the good god of greed is so very, very good.

It was Ayn Rand's belief that the self is paramount, primary, and dominant. She encouraged her followers to become absorbed and preoccupied with themselves in an excessive and obsessive manner. This approach to themselves helped them become self-sufficient, self-fulfilled, self-reliant, and self-actualized as well as self-determined and self-realized.

The culture determines our beliefs and values. It governs our behaviors. Our understanding of what it means to be a human being flows from our beliefs, values, and behaviors. The belief that man is a rational animal inculcates in each of us the moral call to be conscious and to think. In answering the call to think, I am mandated to be responsible for my life. It is up to me to function in a way that I make my life happen. This is done by committing myself to the values of performing, achieving, and succeeding. In doing this, I will arrive at my place of glory in having the ability to be self-determined, self-sufficient, and self-actualized as a rational, thinking human being.

Ayn Rand's philosophy was anchored in individualism. Her worldview placed the individual as the center of power in the culture, establishing the individual as solely responsible for making and directing his life. This leads the individual to become and to be a narcissistic person. This way of being co-mingles with the capitalistic understanding of human living, which completes the striving of being all you can be. Adopting the capitalistic style of being and living will now lead me to participate in happiness. When day is done, I go to bed only to find myself tossing and turning, worrying about how my prosperity will be tomorrow.

Implicit in this success story is that people are gods who must be open and true to themselves and take responsibility for everything that happens to them. From this perspective, it is believed that to get along and get ahead in this competitive age you have to be fit, ambitious, ruthless, and relentless.

It is of the utmost importance that you believe in yourself. Self-esteem is your ticket to making you a fitter, better, and victorious contestant in the neoliberal game of becoming the ideal perfect self and hero. Ayn Rand's heroic person is extroverted, slim, individualistic, and optimistic, a hardworking, popular, socially aware individual with high self-esteem and entrepreneurial spirit. In following economic capitalism, Rand encouraged people to participate in the noblest activities of high productivity and achievement.

Our commitment to the ideal self is a commitment to the cultural values. We, as individuals, get strokes from the culture. We are raised up as the culture starts dancing and cheering that we have swallowed the Kool-Aid. The culture nourishes us with praise and other emotional resources as a reward for being the ideal self that they have convinced us to be. They have created a false self for us to wear and now we don't know what is really ours and what is the cultural mandate.

While all this is going on consciously, the body knows the difference. The narcissist had or has had deformative periods of observing, being exposed, or feeling inadequate, impotent, or worthless. Other experiences could include being controlled, dominated, feeling less than, or taken over. As a result, we may say to ourselves, "This will not happen to me again!"

We then develop a whole worldview of rational-self-interest to make sure that we are never humiliated. We defend ourselves and put up barriers to protect ourselves from being humiliated. We don't want to be in a powerless experience again. We feel that we could not bear that sense of humiliation. As a result, we set out to develop a worldview that tries to maintain power over our lives. We are committed to being in total charge of our lives; believing that the practice of rational self-interest will save the day for us.

Control serves the same function as power. They are two sides of the same coin. They work together to protect the individual from feeling vulnerable and powerless in order to prevent the possibility of feeling humiliation.

The Gospel of Prosperity

We have focused upon a reflection of the American culture and in particular the American Dream. In being open to the worldview of the American way of life, we have uncovered a set of attitudes, values, and goals that have become obstacles to the unfolding of the disposition of hospitality in our culture. The image of a stethoscope may assist us in listening to the pulsations of the culture.

Listening with our stethoscope and magnifying the portrait of the culture reveals that a particular style of the functional dimension of human living disconnects us from our bodies and covers over the spirit dimension of awe, wonder, and mystery in our lives.

Our bodies become numb, anesthetized, and physically exhausted. Hecticness is a way of life. We get caught up in a great sleep and get lost in a feeling of being half-awake and half-asleep as we move about our everyday activity.

The economic gospel of consumption and the accumulation of abundance create a tension of puffing up our image of performing, producing, and achieving success to become a winner. Incivility, disrespect, and a failure to recognize the dignity of the other stand out as obstacles to hospitality in our culture. Greed and rational self-interest corrupt the soul of the culture. Striving to control, to dominate and possess who and what is around us hardens our hearts, blocks our ears, and shuts our eyes. Seeking comfort and security gives us a false sense of functioning well in our world. Our spirit becomes damaged. Awe, wonder, and mystery are replaced by the shining objects that advertisers promise will mend our souls, fill us up with empty calories, and drive us into the promised land of happiness.

In the American culture, there is a preoccupation with amassing wealth and raising our standard of living. There is an insatiability and a feverish drive for self-improvement and security. Although society has been established primarily for the purpose of guaranteeing food and protection, the culture is driven by the needs to achieve, compete, and profit while increasing mobility and expansiveness.

Getting ahead, rising on the social scale, and outstripping others has propelled our industrial culture to rely on molding and shaping its citizens' consciousness by creating new wants and needs through advertising and salesmanship, manipulating and seducing people to believe that they can have it all if they just buy this product. The objective is to create more needs, more desires so that people become motivated to consume it all. The formula is to get into the brain of the customer and condition the mind that they absolutely need this product to advance themselves in the pursuit of being declared successful. Once the need is implanted in the body, the desire is triggered to satisfy the need and the drive toward security.

Fear infuses the closing pitch. Humiliation is the loudest drumbeat. People are hooked to believe that if they fail in the competition of achieving, producing, and expanding, they will be shamed and humiliated. The fear of being degraded and dismissed with contempt because they have not measured up to the standard of virility and masculine self-dependence can become numbing. Fear impels us to maximize our production. To fail in this worldview is humiliating, and it murders one's soul.

Mid-twentieth century, white American masculinity took on a particular pulsation in the culture. John Ford, a Hollywood movie director, molded and shaped John Wayne characters into an intimidating, fearless strongman for men to model themselves after. John Wayne became the idealized American muscular hero, mythical warrior, rugged soldier, spirited "bad ass." The masculine soul was to achieve the iconic posture of the rugged individual, fully in command. Aphorisms such as "saddle up," "lock and load," and "true grit" were employed to convey an air of invincibility.

Fearless, tough-as-nails, and one who never backs down were phrases that characterized this posture. Maximized manhood, machismo, being "man enough" was always the goal in a culture where being a wimp was to be erased forever.

The gospel of prosperity was the real selling point. The possibility of achieving economic riches was the hook. A man was expected to take his proper place in the tradition of patriarchy and wield his power over his subservient wife and others on his way into the land of riches.

The original gospel of Jesus was corrupted. The white evangelical teachers and preachers corrupted, degraded, and altered the original words of Jesus. They participated in a disintegration, a degeneration, and an impairment of virtue. The original message of Jesus was translated into a refrain that glorified the egotistic dimension of being human. Competition and conquest facilitated domination.

The functional dimension of existing in the world emphasizes doing, performing, and producing. In our culture, it is the primary way of being. People have been persuaded that they get more for their buck by cultivating a living style that emphasizes a functional over a spiritual way of existing.

A consequence of choosing the functional as our primary way of living is that we abandon our bodies and cover over the sacred. Unable to feel the ground of the sacred under our feet, our energy easily drifts to our head. Various ideologies can drive our everyday activities.

Greed, rational self-interest, and narcissism lead the parade. This deformative ignorance is a perspective that we fall into, absorb, and allow to guide us. Our living is characterized by disrespect, ignorance, and indecency.

Through this intoxication of the egoic, we become lost in thoughtlessness, cynicism, and passionate ambitions. Our unredeemed way of not seeing the other, not hearing the stranger, not connecting with the different one, dominates our way of being in the world. The sacred is corrupted. Amorality takes over our lives. Fraud, fake, and violence are not just part of our vocabulary, they are lived out in our actions. We become part of the mean world, taking down the other, the other who does not belong to our tribe.

Our humanity eroded, service and sacrifice are no longer at the top of our list of virtues. Compassion, responsibility, and generosity are not the dominating values of the day. Being transactional seems to be winning the day.

Is there any room for hospitality in an American culture where loving your neighbor as yourself is not in the headlines?

Resurrecting the Value of Hospitality

The common good is still alive in the culture. The ancient impulse to extend hospitality to the stranger is quietly pulsating. It may take the use of that stethoscope to hear it. It's there, ready to be called forth as a strong cultural value that is practiced in our everyday lives.

Human consciousness is accented by remembering and forgetting, openness and closedness. The culture needs the disposition of hospitality to be uncovered, listened to, and repossessed as a powerful human stance toward the visitor, the guest, the sacred one.

Values of love, truth, sacredness, generosity, and respecting the need for solitude for the other are foundations of the Western culture. Our American national character has been committed to the common good. Kindness, honesty, frankness, decency, simplicity, and gentleness have influenced the world of family and friendly intimacy. Values are merely ideas about good human relations. Living out these values in our everyday lives can be very foundational and formative for our cultural unfolding of the human experience of hospitality.

Resurrecting the value of hospitality within our American culture would be tremendously helpful in transforming our culture into a more human and humane way of living with each other.

– 4 –
Welcome

My friend, Wally, tells the story of walking up the front stairs of his Aunt Frances's house and ringing the doorbell. All of a sudden, his elderly aunt slowly pulled the edge of the curtain back to peek out to see who was at her door. Her face was filled with big-eyed surprise, gladness, excitement, and a smile that exuded happiness, joy, and aliveness. His Italian aunt could not wait to open her door and welcome her nephew with a warm hug and an affectionate kiss. Wally and his Aunt Frances experienced eye-contact, a smile, a hug, and a lot of affection between them in the moment.

Hospitality is a disposition of welcome, encouragement to make yourself at home in order to rest and be yourself. I would like to dig deeper into the understanding of this experience. Welcome is the first note in the music of hospitality. What is this experience of welcome? It is a well-come, a come and be well. Aunt Frances said to Wally, "Come and be well with me." This strong exclamation, this powerful utterance, this proclamation of "come and be well" is what the experience of welcome is about.

To welcome is to meet, greet, invite, and receive the other. In welcome, the other is saluted, ushered in, appreciated, and embraced. The process of welcoming is an experience of being pleased, gratified, and heartened. The experience of welcome is embodied in a human being. It is a person who welcomes. Aunt Frances was not floating in mid-air as she peeked out from behind the curtain at her door and saw Wally. She was embodied in her welcome. Her excitement, joy, and delight were grounded in the moment of seeing, of hearing, of welcoming her nephew. It is a deep, visceral experience. Her eyes, her voice, her entire body expressed, gestured, exclaimed her gleefulness, her heartwarming pleasure that Wally had come to visit her. Encompassing all her emotions, her body welcomed her guest and said, "Come and you will be well."

As welcomer, Aunt Frances offered Wally comfortable space and time in her home, her personal space. Gifted with a vital aliveness, she also was blessed with the ability, the competence to render hospitality to Wally. Over time, she welcomed many to her home. Her soulful welcome was like a fine wine savored by her guests.

Aunt Frances welcomed Wally over the threshold into her space. Her welcome was not demanding, abrupt, or hectic. Rather, her welcome was patient, humble, and unpretentious. In the moment of welcome, Aunt Frances was filled with care, kindness, generosity, and warmth. In her gracious openness to Wally, she bowed her head out of respect for her nephew, her sister's son. Her bond with her sister was very strong. With respect and reverence to her extended family members, she received Wally with great gratitude. Wally was part of her clan, her people, her tribe. He was part of her close-knit family structure.

As she welcomed Wally, she perceived him as a sacred soul she would wait upon. Her soulfulness toward Wally emerged from the bond she had with her extended family. He was blood of her blood. He was connected to all the ancestors from the old country, the roots of her roots. In honoring Wally, she honored her relatives and their story of coming to America to start a new life, a life of opportunity for prosperity, happiness, and peace.

Aunt Frances in her welcome was focused in the here and now of the moment. In being with Wally, she found herself slowing down, abiding, dwelling, and passing the time with her nephew.

Age had mellowed her. Her experience helped her to become more laid back. She became richer, fuller, tender, and sweet. She was able to bestow herself in a more gracious hospitality that welcomed Wally, inviting him to make himself at home in order to rest and be himself.

In reflecting on the characters in previous chapters, namely, Aunt Sunny, Mémé and Pépé, Nonna, Julie Country Day School, and Aunt Frances, I see that all were engaged in the practice of the art of welcoming others.

They possessed the skill of welcoming. More importantly, they came to embody the *presence* of welcome.

These artists of welcoming invited their guests to cross over the bridge into their homes. They made themselves available. Their homes and Julie Day were places of welcome that were filled with attentive care and concern.

The welcomer hears the knock, the voice of the other, the humanness of the guest. The visitor requests entry, a coming into the space of the welcomer. The welcomer makes available her presence in the here and now of the moment to the guest. She receives the guest from a place of having let go of her egoic self-importance, self-interest, and ego striving. She offers an intimate participation in her being.

Welcoming is a way of being present to another. The focus of this presence is to connect with the other, make contact, and join with the other.

The movement of welcome is a moving toward and a reaching out. To welcome means to be open, meet, and receive the other. It is a willingness to receive and take in the other. In the welcome there is an extending, a stretching toward the other. It is a response of hearing, of seeing the other, of letting it be known that the other is there, at the threshold, the boundary of the situation.

The welcomer's ability to be receptive, open, and welcoming is based on her capacity to be receptive, open, and welcoming to herself. This implies a history, a story of being received and welcomed by another.

Welcoming is an opening up rather than a constricting or a closing. It is a being in harmony, balanced, and centeredness with self and other. Welcoming is a type of presence that is characterized by gentleness, tenderness, and discretion. It is listening closely and carefully.

To welcome the other is being in readiness to respond fully to the other as guest. It is the ability to be still, waiting in silence, and attending to the presence of the guest.

In welcoming the guest, the welcomer offers her space. This space is a living presence. It speaks. It manifests itself. It shows itself. A welcomer invites the guest to experience dignity, worth, and value in her presence. Her welcoming face calls the guest to experience aliveness, pleasure, and joy.

The welcomer's face touches the spirit of the guest. Feeling at home in herself, the welcomer reaches out to her guest and connects with the spirit of the guest. The aliveness of the guest connects with the aliveness of the welcomer. The door to the home of the welcomer is opened. The face of the welcomer beckons the guest, and the guest feels the call to enter, crossing the threshold and finds his way into the interiority of the space of the welcomer.

The welcomer offers her presence to her guest. Her presence is a sense of welcoming. It is a spiritual availability. The availability is rooted in active intimacy with oneself and with the guest.

The welcomer knows from her experience that she is incomplete without others. She senses that she needs to be in a process of actively giving and opening of herself to others. Receiving the stranger, the guest, is to invite and admit the other into intimate participation into the welcomer's being.

The welcomer says to the guest, "*Chez moi*, come into my home, my place." The welcomer's home is her inner space into which the other is welcomed, received, and admitted.

The host responds to the guest's knock on her door. She receives the guest as a sacred one. The welcomer is attentive to the sacredness of the guest. She lets go of whatever she is doing and responds to her guest out of her being rather than her doing. Instead of holding the welcoming situation tightly, she relaxes, surrenders, and gives herself over to the presence of her guest.

She listens, watches, and waits. She pays attention, gives and receives. She bubbles up with sincere, gracious presence. She is released from her ordinary activities and becomes full of love, warmth, comfort, and receptivity for her guest.

The welcomer has been in a process of embracing her weaknesses, brokenness, vulnerability, and her deepest, darkest secrets. This enables her to reach out and respond to the guest's weakness, brokenness, and vulnerability. The mutual recognition of each other's precious, vulnerable selves allows for a connecting as fellow travelers in life.

The welcomer receives her guest with gladness and delight. She takes great pleasure in the presence of her guest. She expresses kind wishes, recognition, good will, and respect. She commends the guest as a person worthy of confidence. The welcomer makes an act of faith in the guest. She believes in the basic goodness of the guest until further notice.

The welcomer finds herself in a "resist nothing" mode of being. She is able to see and accept the guest without judgment as he is in that time and space.

Welcome is a hospitable experience in which one human being, the host, greets, invites, and receives another human being, the guest, with a glad, delighted, and open heart, into her personal space. This reception is a gesture, an expression, a manner by which the host willingly admits and permits the guest into her presence. Welcoming is a letting in, a taking in, an extending to the guest space and time to share and visit with the host. With open arms and reaching hands, the host opens the door of her warm heart to the guest with courtesy, cordiality, and generosity. In the moment of welcome, the host graciously and with pleasure, accepts and affirms the arrival of the guest.

If you are welcoming, you will find peace. As you abide and dwell, you uncover your ground. There, in your grounded stillness, you are awakened to a sense of being helped by something greater than yourself. This powerful otherness feels benevolent.

The image of a flourishing botanical garden comes to mind. It delights and inspires. Even while it raises your spirits, it anchors and roots you deep in the ground. The awe and wonder lift you up and the firmness of the cultivated land holds you up and receives you with welcome.

The welcomer within the present moment is alive, spontaneous, and expressive. She possesses a nobility of character, a distinctive way of being. Secure, firm, and steady, the welcomer is unflappable in her ability to connect with her guest. Her inner contentment and peace of mind allow her to be available, to be truly present to her guest.

In welcoming there is only waiting in patience and trust. The welcomer continues to live from her spirit center. The welcome is unguarded, spontaneous, open, and energetically charged with a radiant glow.

The welcomer practices discretion toward the guest. She is able to be discerning and uses good judgment in assessing the behavior of the guest.

She is unpretentious toward the guest. From a reserved, recollected stance toward the guest, the welcomer remains thoughtful of the other in her solicitation, her attentive care, and concern toward the guest.

Grounded in her body and having confidence in her skill at welcoming, the welcomer has a good foundation to be humble in the face of the guest. The host knows her place, feels comfortable, secure and at home in her space. She is able to keep her hand open to her guest. The welcomer's internal quiet, calm, stillness, open up a posture of letting be, allowing her to be in the present with the guest. The welcomer is able to surrender to the moment as she is grounded in her own person. On the spot, she is able to be her own person. Her heart is pulsating with openness, compassion, and gentleness. Acquired stillness and peacefulness permeate the situation.

Having invested time and energy into helping herself become at home in herself and with herself, she feels secure, grounded, and experiences a sense of well-being.

Over time, the welcomer has come to value and has solidly committed herself to a more leisurely way of life. This means that she has come to hold her everyday life experience lightly. She is sensitive to maintaining a gentle, slowed down pace in which she takes time to abide and dwell in being with herself.

The welcomer prepares and cares for the space in a way that the space invites the guest to rest and be himself. The ambience, the atmosphere of the space was set up based on the welcomer's experience, ideas, vision, and sense of what, indeed, comprises welcoming space.

The welcomer created the space in a way that invited the guest to feel welcomed. She secured the space and attended to the details that expressed her care for the soul of the guest.

The welcomer was able to breathe life into the space. She invited the guest to inhabit the space in a natural, immediate, practical, and personal manner. The welcomer imbued the space with a fullness of life and spirit. The things in the space were properly placed and accented. The whole gestalt of the space drew in, invited, called forth the guest to sit down, settle in, relax, and just be.

The welcomer guards and protects, watches and keeps safe the welcoming space. She continues to set it apart, keeping it a place of beauty, comfort, and security. In all its splendor, it delights and enchants the soul of the guest. The welcomer radiates a quiet charm, a calm and peaceful stillness, that soothes and tranquilizes the soul.

The welcomer emanates warmth and graciousness. She is able to do and be this because she has received the gift along the way. At some point in her life, she was blessed, formed, and shaped by warmth and graciousness. It is from this original source that warmth and graciousness came into being for her. The welcomer has had a history of being sourced in warmth and graciousness.

The welcomer has been received by a significant other in a way, in a manner that opened up the possibilities of being given and receiving the primordial human experiences of warmth and graciousness.

My wife, Denise, embodies this sense of graciousness. She is kind, warm-hearted, considerate, and thoughtful. These are dimensions of her being. Pleasantness, accommodation, and magnanimity are aspects of her way of being. Compassionate, caring with a beautiful smile and welcoming, soft eyes complete the picture of her graciousness and manner of hospitality.

Welcome! Come and be well! By inviting you into our space, we are hoping and believing that we will be able to meet and greet you, open up our space and invite you to join us in sharing time and space together. In this welcoming style of sharing space and time together, the welcomer opens the possibility for the guest to receive time and experience comfort.

Welcoming is an opening up rather than a constricting or a closing. It is being in harmony, balance, and centeredness with self and other. Welcoming is a type of presence that is characterized by gentleness, tenderness, and discretion. It is listening closely, carefully and being responsibly open to the guest.

To welcome the other is being in readiness to respond fully to the other as guest. It is the ability to be still and wait in silence, attending to the presence of the guest.

The welcomer communicates that the space of her home is a place for the guest to be at home, rest, and be himself. Before the welcomer gracefully signals her guests to enter, she has reflectively, interiorly, collected herself. She has checked her ego at the door. Now, with empty hands, she makes contact, meets, and greets, then invites and receives her guest into her space of welcoming comfort and peace. She does this in a willing, effortless, and self-giving manner.

Being welcomed is a personal interplay between host and guest. The welcomer, the host, offers a sincere, genuine, authentic, and empathic connection to her guest. The welcomer feels a responsibility to protect, shelter, and safeguard the peace and well-being of her guest. She attends to her guest with humility and generosity, gratitude and appreciation that her guest has knocked on her door to visit. She receives the guest at the door and welcomes him, wishing and hoping that the guest can experience being able to come in and be well. With genuine respect, honor, consideration, and kindness, she receives her guest with warmth, care, and generosity. Her keen perception and sharp sensing increase her ability to notice, listen, attend, and respond to her guest in a more easeful and relaxed manner.

The welcomer has become awake and is aware of how the deformative dimension of the American culture has informed and shaped her egoic inclination toward mere performance. She understands and accounts for this, thus her welcome is heartfelt and not mere performance. She remembers to ground herself in the here and now moment of welcoming the guest.

I want to emphasize that being grounded in oneself, not lost in the egoic, is essential to authentic welcome, and in turn, to hospitality.

The welcomer is the fire maker, the builder of the fire, the tender of the fire. On a cold winter night in New England, the guest appreciates walking into the house, greeted by the warming fire in our fireplace. After removing his coat, he immediately stands in front of the fire to warm himself.

Building a fire is both an art and a craft. Steady, persistent heat emerges from the burning coals. The blazing fire is not as steadily warming as is a stack of slow burning coals.

The welcomer, who is interested in impressing his guest with a blazing fire, a bonfire that creates a quick flash of light, shooting flames of fire, will not succeed in the long run of the evening. Not knowing how to build a warm, glowing fire will not serve the guest well. The craft of building a fire is an art as well. Being a welcomer also is an art.

In the hospitality industry, the welcomer, the greeter is functionally well trained. The spirit of the welcomer is not necessarily attended to or valued. The focus is on the quick, the flashy, the blazing fire of the welcomer. The presence of welcomer is not taken into consideration. Fake it until you make it may be the professional welcomer's disposition. The presence of the welcomer is not considered to be important. For example, the welcomer in a restaurant may be better trained in selling the special of the night, rather than focusing on helping the guest to feel warmly greeted and invited into a space where the guest will feel supported and embraced by the pleasure of the dining experience.

I am reminded of an evening about forty years ago. My wife and I were having dinner in a small Italian restaurant in the North End of Boston. Our waiter for the evening was named Michael. What an evening it was!

Michael, a man in his fifties, was our welcomer, who attended, served, and waited upon us. He was a vibrant and energized human being. His eyes sparkled, his smile was radiant. Michael's shining face had a soft, bright glow that conveyed a cheerful, peaceful friendliness. His tone of voice was gentle, warmhearted, and welcoming. His way of speaking manifested a sensitivity and sensibility to us as guests. His movements were gracious, effortless, and easeful. We experienced his presence as respectful, dignified, and reverential toward us. He had a patient, humble, and unpretentious presence about him.

The dining experience that he orchestrated for us was an experience of slowing down, becoming open and receptive to all that was around us and in us. His attentive presence opened up a deeper presence to us, others, and the world around us.

His style was sincere, genuine, natural, and authentic. He carried himself with great ease, self-possession, and assurance of manner. He was of the earth, not in the clouds.

In a thoughtful and caring manner, he created a distinctive atmosphere around the table. He was intentional, deliberate, and disciplined as he attended closely to our feeling of well-being and pleasure.

Michael's care was filled with a soulfulness and generosity of spirit. He conveyed a simplicity, an internal calm, a tranquility, a comfort in his own skin that seemed to enable him to take life in stride, to go with the flow of the concrete situation of following his inner calling of being a waiter, a server of people, whom he embraced with his presence and allowed them to just be.

It was clear that Michael had developed a sense of self-awareness, self-respect, trust, and appreciation of who he was as a human being. His spirit of hospitality and welcome emerged from his warm, open, compassionate, and empathetic heart. He had well-developed sensibilities of kindness, thoughtfulness, care, and concern. His ability to welcome us into his space and time was remarkable and memorable. His welcoming presence was a spiritual blessing. Indeed, he said to us, "Come and be well." It was an experience I will never forget.

Seeing the Guest as Sacred

The story of the unfolding of humanity includes the disposition of hospitality. Within this disposition, we encounter the dynamic of the welcomer and the guest, the host and the stranger. Many traditions name the guest as a holy one. Perceiving the guest from the perspective of religious beliefs, the guest is acknowledged as holy, venerated as sacred. The stranger, the foreigner, the guest needs to be invited into the welcomer's home as the holy one.

With the religious dimension in mind, the welcomer opens the door, lets down his barriers including his armor that has covered his heart and soul and acknowledges, receives, and welcomes the guest as the blessed one. In the art of welcoming, the guest is valued as a mystery to be received as sacred. The welcomer believes that the presence of the mystery resides in the guest. It is in the humanness of the guest that the welcomer finds a place of connection. The welcomer has learned through his life experience that it is through their shared humanness that they will connect. In that space, they meet each other, share each other's presence, and uncover the sacred presence in which they also share and deepen their sense of being human.

The welcomer is a practitioner who is able to invite the guest to come and be well. The welcomer has developed the skills necessary to manifest her disposition of welcoming with kindness, warmth, and respect. She honors her guest with a humble and thoughtful reception. She knows in her soul that it is right and good to respond to and serve the guest who is knocking on the door. Welcoming the guest is a sacred, ancient ritual of receiving the guest with a "Come and be well."

Welcoming is a thinking of the other. It is a seeing of the other. The face is the naked and living presence of the other. When the person begging for money on the street corner looks at me in the face, there is a powerful moment that unfolds. This person wants to be seen, recognized, and connected. His hands are not just reaching out for a charitable contribution but are also—and more importantly—reaching out to my obligation and responsibility toward humankind.

It is in this quick moment that the vulnerability of the other is disclosed and appeals to our common humanity. How is it that I am not the beggar? We share a common story of growing up in America. Facing this needy person, the other, I feel an infinite responsibility toward him. I have a duty to respond.

I find myself in conflict. The cultural pulsation of Ayn Rand reminds me that I am to be for myself; it's all about my self-interest. I am to be for myself before being for the other. I need to treasure the values of greed and profit. But the hand of the beggar, and more emphatically his face, calls out the responsibility to protect and serve the needs of others, the other. I am reminded to recognize the divinity that this beggar shares.

This moment of the beggar looking into my face reminds me that I am in an ethical relationship with this person. His face calls me to give to and serve the other. His face is an expression of a living presence that speaks to me of vulnerability and eminence. His presence before me, his need, proclaims the fragility of the human.

As I stay with that moment of how we share in human vulnerability and fragility, I feel a welling up of humility. I am called to remember that I am creature, not creator. The priority of obligation and responsibility in the ethical relationship, the insatiable primacy of the other, calls me to be a man for others, a man of service to the other, who sees, who makes contact with me, at the corner of South Main and Hammond streets.

The needy person on this corner, the anonymous, the stranger, the homeless seems to lack a face. But as he passes my car with his sign, "just a dollar will do," we are face-to-face.

His face catches my face, his eyes catch my eyes, and wake me up in the moment. I see in this instant, face-to-face, a young man who looks tired, worn out, exhausted. This stranger, this face, maybe trying to manipulate me to give him a dollar, but something else is also unfolding.

Awakened by his stare, I see the other, then myself. We have made contact. For a split second, our presences meet. He is outside. I am inside. He experiences the rain, the snow, the cold, the hot rays of the blazing sun. He is exposed. I am enclosed.

Our stories are so different. He is the outsider living on the edge, the margin, living from hand-to-mouth. I am living comfortably. He has fallen on hard times. I am enjoying a pleasant life, at least for this moment.

His face speaks. Do I have the courage to let his face speak to me? I can insulate myself from his face. I can order in my mind, don't look at me. But this is just denying that I am always and already in relation with him. There is something in me from which I cannot break away. I must respond to the summons of his pleading face. My heart is still beating. I am not hardened of heart. I am not armored against his stare. He sees me and I see him. I am not protected against his reaching out to me.

His soul, although covered over by choices he has made in his life, is still sending out distress signals looking for help, assistance, aid. His soul reaches out for resuscitation. He wants to be rescued from dying. He needs a spark of life to survive and be brought back to from the edge. Centered on himself, he is lost.

The face of the beggar shocks but also awakens and teaches. I can get lost in my self-concern, my thoughtless self-indulgence, which will assist me in forgetting and suppressing a response to the panhandler, the stranger, the alien one. Or the face-to-face contact with the other can call me to a responsibility toward him. I can embrace the needy person as my teacher, who awakens me to my obligation to be for the other. In catching sight of the face of the other, the beggar, I am awakened from my self-absorption into hospitality.

The stranger, the panhandler, is a gift. His presence disturbs being-at-home-with-myself. He interrupts my complacency, my ability to take for granted that all will be well for me. His presence reminds me that I am ethically responsible and obligated to respond to his call for aid. I owe him my generosity to help him subsist.

The beggar's face speaks of a primordial demand for moral respect. In his begging gaze toward me, he asks for recognition, acknowledgement that he has been seen by me. He reaches out to me, knocks on my car window, and asks that I recognize the claim on his space. He is hungry and needs to eat. He is thirsty and needs to drink.

I am always responsible to the stranger. Ethically, I cannot shirk my responsibility for the stranger whom I encounter in the here and now.

To be an ethically responsible human being is to welcome the stranger into my space, my place, where I offer him hospitality. To do this, I need to let go of my egoism, my focus on myself and my situation. I need to turn my face toward the other.

– 5 –
Make Yourself at Home

Hospitality is a disposition; it is a particular way of being that welcomes another and invites that other to make themselves at home in order to rest and be themselves. "To make themselves at home" is what we will explore next in our search to understand the experience of hospitality.

What does this familiar, everyday, informal colloquialism mean?

Making a home that is prepared to receive a guest. It is laying out, putting together, setting in order the components that constitute the landscape that offers the guest the possibility of being at ease, relaxed, and comfortable.

When an artist paints a painting, they are not driven by their ego to achieve the creation. The writer does not push and pressure themselves to put out their words, to compose their piece of personal expression. If they do, they run the risk of writer's block, a contraction, a restraining of their free expression.

In trying too hard to paint or write, the artists can easily jam up, block up the creative energy from flowing and allowing the piece of art, the process of creating, to come into being.

Creating is a gentle process of bringing something into existence. It is a setting out to do something, but in a certain way. This manner of creating something to happen, to cause something to be, to produce as a result of action, effort, and behavior is not a willful process but a willing process. It is an attempt on the creator's part to ally himself with the gift of willingness. This is an inclining and favoring of a disposition of readiness. The person creating gives himself over to a process of openness, allowing himself to remain receptive to inspiration.

Creating is a willingness to slow down and wait for breath to influence, move, and guide. The maker permits himself to collect his thoughts and feelings, focusing on allowing the creative movement to unfold and express itself in words, paintings, or any other creative endeavors.

Making is not a willfulness. It is a willingness. Making is a holding lightly. It is a gesture of relaxed invitation. It is respectful encouragement to allow oneself to be massaged by the situation. The guest freely gives in to the host's guidance to surrender to the moment of being welcomed.

The welcomer is appealing to the spirit dimension of the guest. The welcomer is aware that their guest is a mystery and is part of a mystery of the unfolding of life. The welcomer is being reminded that the guest brings a whole story with them as they enter the room.

The welcomer's words, "Make yourself at home," are friendly and cordial. It is a standard appropriate greeting of a guest.

The welcomer is not requesting that the guest make an all-out effort to make themselves at home, appealing to the guest to let down and let go.

It may not be easy for the guest "to make" themselves comfortable with little effort to enter the space that the welcomer is inviting them to share.

It is important to remember that we all have a past, a story, a history. In the moment of welcoming the guest, we may not be sensitive to the world of the guest, particularly of their past.

My wife and I have invited many people into our home over the years, in particular refugees. Boat people from Vietnam, Iraqi refugees, and immigrants from Central and South America have all accepted our invitation to cross our threshold.

In using the idiom "make yourself at home," we realize it brings up issues of trust, comfortability, and even having a sense of self.

But the human spirit is still present in the guest, who wants to believe that they can give themselves over to this unknown space. They can instantly sense in the welcoming atmosphere that they could give themselves over, but they may want to go very slowly through the process.

That guest possesses a personal openness to what is before them, grounded in the Mystery of Life and unfolding in every moment of every event. Rooted in being awake and aware, they are open to listening to the now of the moment.

As the host, the process requires understanding that I am limited. My limitedness is an invitation to humility, to know my place, to remember my place in the grand scheme of life.

Periodically focusing on our style of welcome, as in making the home welcoming to guests, can keep us honest about how we are taking up welcoming. Asking, is it consistent with a more effortless way of going about preparation, or are we caught up in the willfulness of desperately trying to make it happen in our own egoic manner?

Welcome! Make yourself at home is a figure of speech, a form of expression, a colloquialism. As a way of speaking, the reference to *yourself* is a way of identifying the guest. The expression acknowledges that *yourself* is a person, an individual. As such, the guest is unique, original, and true. They are the origin of what they think, feel, say, and do.

As a human being, *yourself* is a precious, fragile, vulnerable self. Precious means that *yourself* is of great value, highly esteemed, and cherished. As a vulnerable person there is a certain fragility to the other, to *yourself*, which the welcomer knows means to handle the other carefully.

Yourself—as in make yourself at home—is the person who is embodied, is able to function, and is inspired by spirit. On the vital/bodily level of existence, the guest is able to come in, be received into a space, and take a seat. They know how to conduct themselves socially and have the skills to be a proper guest. An aliveness streams through their body as their spirit is honored by the manner in which they are received by their welcomer.

Let us proceed to the last phrase of our colloquialism, which is *at home*. In the summer of 1961 in Leominster, Massachusetts, Wally and his friend, Carl, were sitting around Wally's house one afternoon.

Over the years, Wally had experienced his mother, Gracie, as being a truly hospitable person. It was clear Gracie welcomed everyone into her home.

Over the years, Gracie's mother asked her, "Why do Americans ask people what they would like to eat or drink? You only ask sick people what they want to eat or drink."

The custom in Italy was that food and drink were put on the table and guests would be invited to help themselves.

When Wally and his friend, Carl, came into her house, Gracie, would immediately in a warm, friendly, gracious manner, immediately offer to Carl a beverage and snack from her refrigerator.

One day Wally and Carl came into the kitchen when Gracie happened to be on the second floor. Carl helped himself to whatever he wanted in the refrigerator.

"As you know my mother was never reluctant to use street language and many expletives in her everyday speaking, to the delight of my friends," Wally said as he relayed this story. None of them were accustomed to hearing their mothers use such obscene or profane words expressed with such strong feeling. Never a wallflower, Gracie would not shy away from using colorful street language if she was upset, angry, or irritated. When she felt injured, used, or abused, she would make herself known, her voice clear, direct, loud, and powerful.

Gracie came down from the second floor to greet Wally and Carl and discovered that Carl had taken food from her refrigerator. Angry, she said, "Who the hell gave you permission to go into my refrigerator without asking me? If you want something, just tell me."

Once Carl left, Wally suffered the repercussions. Gracie asked Wally, "Why did you let Carl go into the refrigerator and help himself without my permission?"

Wally shared with me that being a teenager and always in search of others' approval, he would react with a penitent face to his mother, but never said anything to his friend.

The way the ill-mannered teenager made himself at home was a miscalculation of the situation. Carl's behavior displayed an indifference to good form, a departure from the common manners of being a guest. His moment of being unpolished and lacking grace was seen as evidence that he was thoughtless, narcissistic, and impulsive. While Gracie was a gracious hostess, there were boundaries to that hospitality. When she would say, "Make yourself at home," she did not mean that you could invade, raid, or trespass.

At Home

Hospitality is a process of welcoming others to make themselves at home. I have tried to articulate the meaning of the experiences of welcome, make, and yourself. The notion of *at home* is my next offering.

This space called home is a place, a physical, concrete structure. This shelter, enclosure, private domain, is a place, a center of significance, that we have carved out in our situation of living our everyday lives. In this space, we inhabit, reside, and dwell.

As a sanctuary, a home is a solid ground to stand on, a zone of protection, a sacred space. It is a place that has been humanized. This means that it is a familiar, warm, comfortable space where we feel safe, secure, and grounded. We are able to rest, settle in and become centered. As we inhabit, spend time, and quiet down, we find ourselves letting down, letting go, and simply being.

Home-making is an active process of taking care in the structuring and preservation of one's dwelling. Being-at-home is facilitated by becoming at home with oneself. The more I am able to accept, respect, and revere who I am, the more I find myself attuned to my body, and there uncover, discover, and recover my personal foundation of my at-homeness.

Living in my body in a particular manner assists me in finding a sense of being at-home in the moment, in the here and now. It is an experience of becoming aware of, being present to, my body such that I gain access to my body, connect, and can be awake to the inner life that resides there. This consciousness that I am awake, aware, and attend to my experience helps me become present to coming home to myself more intentionally, more explicitly, more directly. Noticing my breathing, I find myself connecting to a space within that I call *home*. Abiding in this space, I feel a sense of homecoming. This experience of embodiment opens a return, a settling into this wonderful place, and feeling of at-homeness within myself.

This experience of at-homeness is a resting, an abiding, a dwelling within myself. It is a letting reality be. In this moment, I feel connected to myself, belonging to myself, having faith in myself. In and through this moment, I feel rooted, grounded, and in possession of myself.

Peace, contentment, and joy emerge. I feel connected to my heart and soul. A wave of feeling held by the sacredness of life brings me into an experience of gentleness. I am gently embraced by the feeling of being-at-home in myself and in the world around me.

This moment of at-homeness has slowly developed into a way of being. Over time, this way of being has become more consistent, more thematic, a more embedded part of my consciousness.

The expression *being at home* is not an act of doing, but an act of being. It is a way of existing in the moment or for a period of time, a style of being within one's self. One can be at home in one's bed, in one's house, in one's town.

Being at home can be a manner, a style of human consciousness. It is a way of being present to a person, event, or thing. As a style of human presence, we conduct ourselves in a certain mode of being. In being at home, I do not make myself do something. Rather, I find myself called into this manner of being.

The experience of being at home is an intimacy of place. It is an atmosphere that emerges between myself and the situation. The situation could be a person, place, or thing. I could find myself being at home in my body, with myself, with certain people around me, in a particular chair, space, garden, or eating a meal with family or friends.

I remember knocking on the back door of Uncle Peter's house. Through the door, I heard a welcome. Uncle Peter was genuine, authentic, and kind in his invitation to come and be well. As I heard his voice saying, "Come in," I discerned a striking manifestation of gentleness and appreciation. I felt welcome to come in and visit.

Uncle Peter opened the door and with a big smile, excitement in his eyes and voice, offered me a seat at his kitchen table. I felt an immediate connection to him and his home. Within seconds, I felt at home.

What happened in this moment so that I felt that *at-homeness* flood the room? Uncle Peter was an ordinary man with an extraordinary presence.

What was his magic, his ability to be part of the experience such that I found myself steeped in the feeling of at-homeness?

Looking back at the at-homeness experience in Uncle Peter's kitchen on the corner of Sixth and Lancaster Streets in Leominster, Massachusetts, there was a timelessness in the situation. My consciousness was not present to time, the clocks ticking are not part of the memory. Rather, there was a simple living in the moment, being in the here and now. There was no past nor future. There was just the now, an attunement to the present moment.

I was not riveted to time, not trying to beat the clock, not controlled by time. I was not trying to live by schedules or deadlines. I felt slowed down, taking one step at a time.

Being at-home means that I felt comfortable and at ease. Acceptance of myself was foundational to this moment or state of being at-home. Uncle Peter's affirming presence added to the naturalness of simply letting down, letting go, and feeling a sense of peace in the moment.

I was not in my head thinking, calculating, or trying to figure it all out. Trying too hard was not my way of being in the moment.

Making peace with myself, my limitations, and the mystery of who I am allowed me to relax, be gentle, kind, and patient with myself.

As Uncle Peter cleared space for me to be with him, inviting me to be at home in his space, I came to honor myself as he honored me. Being honored, I felt more and more comfortable and at ease and continued to let go of any residue of the egoic in me and took my proper place in his welcoming space. I allowed his blessing and anointing to facilitate the feeling of being at-home as it quietly filled me up and allowed me to just be.

At-homeness is that depth of peace found in a special place where I feel accepted and loved for who I am, rather than what I do. It is a space where I feel comfortable and at ease, confident, and relaxed. It is a place to dwell and abide.

In my acceptance of myself, my limitations, and incompleteness are affirmed. I feel at one with myself; I belong to myself and reconcile myself with my real self. I admit that I am powerless and have no control. When I surrender to the deeper truth of my reality, I feel at peace and at home with who I am.

At-homeness is a feeling of being at ease. This means that I am free from worry, awkwardness, or problems. I am relaxed. In being at ease, I can feel serene, calm, tranquil, contented, and comfortable. There is an effortlessness, a naturalness; I am at peace.

Being at-ease is to perceive the world as safe and trustworthy until further notice. The guest's body relaxes into a condition where it is obvious, especially to the host, that the guest is taking it easy. The person feels, and is perceived, as unencumbered by anything distressing in relationship with self, other, and the world. The perception that one is safe and can trust that safety is essential to becoming at ease.

The descriptions of hospitality in Chapter Two all manifested a sense of being at home. The architecture of the Arts and Crafts home was created with the hope that its residents would experience a sense of at-homeness, comfort, and peace. That is what I experienced at 42 Academy Road.

My Nonna's house also was a sanctuary, a sacred space in which I felt familiar, warm, comfortable, and at home. Julie Country Day School was a place where I experienced a sense of being able to let down, let go, and simply be. I felt very at-home and at ease walking and exploring the magnificent grounds of Julie Country Day.

The experience of at-homeness is supported by our ability to be in our bodies and function in a way that enables our spirits to be in the moment and align ourselves with what is around us that allows us to let go, let down, let be and be ourselves. Making a guest comfortable, at ease, and feeling they are safe and secure, at home, and at peace is the goal of the host offering hospitality.

Feeling comfort, at peace, at ease, at home, I experience a tranquility, a quietude, an utter calm. At-homeness with myself facilitates a gratitude, a thankfulness that opens me up to awe, wonder, and mystery. My self-possession of spirit enables me to deepen my respect and reverence for all that I encounter.

As we welcome the guest and request that they make themselves at home, we perceive the guest as a sacred soul whom we wait upon. The heart of the welcomer is filled with care, compassion, generosity, and warmth.

In the welcomer's gracious openness to the guest, they deeply bow to the guest in gentle humility.

It is the host, the welcomer, conveying, radiating, emanating graciousness to the guest, the visitor, that is the extent to which the guest is likely to feel safe enough to relax, be at ease, and make themselves at home. The graciousness of the welcomer conveys a sense of trustworthiness to the guest.

The gracious host, with their warm sense of welcoming, is consistent and sincere in inviting the guest to be at ease and make themselves at home. The welcomer's invitation to come and be well frees the guest to let go and just be in the moment with their host, who is inviting them to let go of their uncertainty, apprehension, preoccupation with lists of shoulds and musts.

The host invites the guest to have faith, confidence, and trust in their welcoming presence. It is a presence in which the guest can feel safe enough to relax, be at ease, and make themselves at home. The presence of the welcomer conveys a sense of trustworthiness to the guest.

The guest comes from elsewhere, another place that is outside of the welcomer's space. The welcomer knows and is sensitive to the fact that the guest came from an outside space into the inside space of the host. The welcomer has the gift, the ability to assist the guest to let down and let go, to feel comforted by the inside space. There the guest feels free, at ease and at home.

– 6 –

Rest

For more than fifty years, the quaint, charming village of Ogunquit, Maine has been a place where my wife and I go to relax in our leisure time. Walking east, up Shore Road is a small, pointed sign indicating the direction of the Marginal Way. If you were an uninformed tourist, you might dismiss it as leading to another group of rental cottages. That would be a major mistake. The sign marks both the beginning of and direction to a slender 1.25-mile magnificent winding path of wind-blown gorgeousness that edges the Atlantic Ocean.

The tarred path hugs the rocky edge of a small cliff and winds down and around rocky flats. Along this scenic coastal walk are thirty-nine comfortable benches. These weather- worn benches are smooth from thousands of people sitting on them while taking in the beautiful three-mile stretch of sandy beach and dunes in the distance.

The benches are placed strategically along the scenic, coastal walk. Each bench seems to act as a private oasis where people become still and dwell within the panorama before them. Once people sit on a bench and are drawn into gazing at what is before them, they let go, let down, and rest. Even the loud jokers walking along the path begin to act as if they have entered a church when they take a seat upon a bench. They quickly become quiet and respectful of the setting.

Each of these pleasant refuges of joy is situated in various rock formations and seacoast flora, which include shady groves, bayberry, honeysuckle, bittersweet, and gnarled shrubs of fragrant pink and white sea roses.

Within the North Atlantic coastal ecological environment of the

Marginal Way, my wife and I simply sit on one of the benches. The expansive views of the breaking waves, the thundering seawater crashing against rocks and spraying out over tide pools, are parts of the inspiring grandeur taken in from our bench.

The fresh smell of the ocean, its swirling and churning waters, the vividness of its multicolored foam, the seaweed, the undulating tidal movements all melt the observer into pure leisure. Over the years, my wife and I have enjoyed seasonal changes, all beautiful and unique. We have even noticed the differences of various times of the day.

Sitting on a bench on this beloved coastal path has been and remains an invitation to experience a depth of leisure. The whole gestalt of what I have described as sitting on a bench on the Marginal Way elicits an attitude of leisure within me. With an empty mind and holding what I am simply observing ever so lightly, I relax and rest.

The Freedom of Leisure

A leisurely walk along the Marginal Way invites us to transcend the world of work. Free from demands, duties, obligations, and responsibilities, the experience of leisure liberates us from being on overload, skating in the roller derby, riding the merry-go-round, or running the rat race. In leisure, we are no longer gripped by fulfilling the practical, the pragmatic, or the utilitarian objectives set out for us.

In leisure, the functional dimension of human living is not our primary way of being present to what is around us. We are not controlled by the managing, doing, mastering, achieving, grasping, striving ways of being. In leisure, we are not focused on what must be done, produced, or accomplished.

The leisurely attitude is not focused on being purposeful, making things happen, being geared up, making ready for running an efficient and effective operation.

In the experience of being leisurely, we are not overly consciously ruled by time. We are at peace with time. Time is our own. There are no pressures, stresses, or intrusions on our time. We are living free time, not working time.

In leisure time, time does not control us. We are not concerned about wasting time or that we should be busy, doing something with our time. Instead, in the experience of leisure, we feel that we have no worries or concerns in the world. There is carefreeness in our taking time to give ourselves over to the moment of doing nothing.

Leisure is a fundamental attitude toward life. It is a world of purposelessness.

In enjoying leisure, we are free from the tyranny of time. There is no pushing, striving, or squeezing in of time. Time is not something to be done to or done with. Leisure time means simply being like a child again and enjoying with a fresh sense of wonder and delight in time.

In leisure time, we slow down and can be still. We let go, let life in, and let it happen. We are able to breathe easier and more deeply and thus increase our quality of life.

Being re-collected and self-possessed becomes more of a possibility through having a more leisurely attitude in everyday life.

Our ego becomes more a humble servant rather than a king in our experience of leisure. In coming to rest in leisure, we are not concerned with being the king of the hill but, rather, with being a more peaceful, open, and receptive soul who finds ourselves growing in appreciation and gratitude. We find ourselves better able to rest and be mindful of the mystery of life in which we find ourselves. We participate in and respond to that life in a more playful, reflective, and celebratory manner.

An Invitation to Rest

Leisure is a foundational disposition of the spiritual life. It slows us down from the hustle and bustle of our everyday life. There, in the moment of the stillness of dawn, the glow of a brilliant sunset, freed from the pressures of the strife of the world, little invitations to a moment of transcendence emerge.

In these moments of holding the reins lightly, loosely, relaxedly, I am able to pause. Ceasing my activity and movement, at ease with reality, I am in the now, yielding, surrendering, and growing still. I patiently find myself available to and disposed toward transcendence. I experience with new eyes and ears the manifestation of transcendence in the world around me. I see the familiar with awe and wonder, as if for the first time.

I am simply present. Watching, waiting, and wondering open up sights, spaces, and situations that invite me to slow down, open my hands, and take up the presence of the transcendence that discloses itself to me in the everyday moments of my life.

Leisure is the willingness to surrender one's life to the transcendent, the sacred, the mystery. In gratitude, I revel in my dependence upon someone greater than myself.

In leisure, I admire and enjoy beauty. It is a pause in which my mind and body become rested and refreshed. Recuperative rest and joyful play deepen my inner harmony.

Hospitality is a process of welcome, inviting a guest to make themselves at home in order to rest and be themselves. Of all these components making up our notion of hospitality, the one that is often least understood is the invitation to rest.

But what do we mean by rest? For most of us, the rest we seek is usually associated with our home, that place—however construed—where we go in search of physical repose. At home, we try to reduce our activities to a minimum in order to take the time necessary to relax.

At home then, we seek to rest from our daily exertions, as we free ourselves from toil, strain, stress, and tension. Pulling back from our engagement with work, we reach for a loosening up, a letting go, a release from physical demands. As we try to give our bodies relief from the hectic, hurried push and pull of our everyday activities, we hope to relinquish at last that daily need to get things done.

All too often in our workplace, we contract our bodies as we overexert ourselves. This bodily tension is most assuredly an obstacle to physical rest. When and if we do physically relax and become less labored, only then do we manage to restore our energy, strength, and power.

Physical repose, however, is but one dimension of rest. Indeed, as we move beyond physical repose, we sense a yearning and a need for emotional rest. That yearning resides in the urge to quiet our emotions, relax our minds, turn down our thoughts, and rest our overstimulated bodies. This urge remains unsatisfied as long as worry, anxiety, and inner noise conspire to deprive us of emotional rest. Quieting our inward activity helps us to come to our senses. Solitude, privacy, and silence allow us then to slowly and naturally sink without effort into emotional rest. And when our emotions find rest, we experience peace and serenity.

Spiritual Rest

The deepest dimension of rest is spiritual. As a state of being, spiritual rest is becoming still, at peace, a contentment of mind and soul. The attainment of spiritual rest invites us to contemplate while remembering that the roots of our true home are in God. The transcendent, the sacred, the mystery beckon us in our weariness to rest in the stillness of His living waters where our soul will be restored.

In spiritual rest, we experience the fullness of life supporting us in every moment. As we rest in being, we dwell in the house of the Lord. All creation becomes our resting place—our home—where we grow in confidence of God's protection, refuge, and strength. As we dwell in that home, we experience God's graciousness and mercy for it is always God who invites us to draw near where rest is given to us.

In spiritual rest then, we remember and experience that God is the Creator upon whom everything depends. We are reminded that everything is the work of a providential God. Such an understanding must lead us to concur with St. Augustine: "Our hearts are restless until they rest in God."[11]

When we rest in God, we are made meek and poor in spirit in the full evangelical sense of the terms. These dispositions help us to live abundantly. Herein we find true rest for our souls. It is a rest that can only yield security and serenity in harmony with the mysterious ground of life. In such a way, we rest in the arms of a loving Father, who is our refuge and fortress. And it is this rest—His rest—which is ultimately the only dependable rest.

Spiritual rest allows us to pause in order to appreciate and experience the presence of God. Mindful of God's presence, we surrender more and

---

11 St. Augustine

more into God's loving embrace. In surrender to rest, we remember that God is our protector and our assurance.

Spiritual rest is therefore surrendered rest. As we pursue our lives in ever increasing meekness, we find that God will give us rest. As we grow in gentleness and humility, we find ourselves ever more capable of enduring injury with patience and without resentment. Moreover, we become more moderate in our actions, gentler in our behaviors. Lack of pretense becomes more pronounced. Thus, we are more who we really are—precious, fragile, and vulnerable selves. In this way, we accept full vulnerability as we empty ourselves and enter into God's fullness.

Only when our full surrender is complete in the acceptance of God's law will our soul find true rest. Only then will we experience the blessed relief that comes from self-acceptance devoid of pretense.

The Toll of Living Outside Ourselves

Living in a culture that all too often pressures us to live outside of ourselves, we are systematically urged to become "externally referenced." That is, we adopt an external standard when measuring our internal sense of self-worth. As a result, others' attitudes and judgments assume far too much importance in forming our sense of self-esteem. In purely personal terms, what people think of us takes hold and exerts a formidable pressure.

We develop an excessive dependency on the public eye, a focus too concentrated on measuring and comparing ourselves to others. We fall prey to the demands of how we should and must live. In the end, many of our thoughts, beliefs, and expectations impede us from being ourselves. This then leads us to the risk of believing we don't measure up, or worse that we are inferior and just not good enough. This can lead us to become self-conscious and fearful that we won't be chosen, included, affirmed, or rewarded. We may tend to worry as we grow anxious, fearful, angry, resentful, and impatient.

Meanwhile, a great many of us in this culture have come to think, believe, and expect that our life's primary focus and greatest human efforts should be anchored in doing, performing, and achieving — in brief, in producing to reach success. Such an approach to life remains too narrowly focused on satisfying obligations, fulfilling duties, and meeting responsibilities.

All this is most often part of our preoccupation with job, income, status, position, and power. When this happens, an excessive exertion of effort becomes our very way of being. And so, it is that we push, pull, drive, press, and pressure ourselves to maximize our output. This addiction to effort is, in effect, situated in a deeper addiction to that fear of falling behind and thus failing at whatever we do.

Preoccupied above all with our images, we find ourselves caught in constant, compulsive activity as we overexert ourselves in attempts to do whatever it will take to quiet our anxieties and insecurities. Corralling our will to gain acceptance—in reaction to our fear of failure, we find ourselves ensnared into increasing our labors as we struggle to push ourselves through life.

Despite this, fleeting moments of self-awareness emerge. We may question, for example, why are we gripping the car's steering wheel so tightly, grasping our cell phones so intensely, pounding the keyboards on our electronic devices, snatching the saltshaker, spilling our beverages, plopping down hard into our chairs, or talking at the much-too-fast-a-pace of our racing minds? In similar instances, we may be overtaken by unnecessarily complicated and constantly noisy chatter filling our heads. At times, we open doors a bit too forcefully, misplace our keys, bump into things, or walk at either much too brisk or too leaden a pace.

In all these circumstances, our relationship to time is one of struggle, a race against time's swift advance. Our uneasiness with time's relentless pace takes over and can consume us just as our overarching concerns with urgency and immediacy tie us in knots. Determined to make every minute count, we constantly strive to beat the clock. To do so, we are obliged to accelerate, race, and rush through our days. Thus, the days fall victim to overdrive, which leads to an existence of non-stop movement. Never do we feel we have enough time. Because of this constant race against the clock, we experience our days as full of stress and strain.

What often results from all of this is living outside of ourselves. This occurs because of our attempts to squeeze more and more time from the day to prove and improve ourselves. Such strivings may contribute to an increase in our vulnerability and a decrease in our own personal power. That is, we may experience an ever-greater detachment from — and betrayal of — our very bodies. Our hectic style and pace of life and our externally referenced way of living create tensions that unleash stress and strain on our bodies. We may begin to grow tight, which often translates into feelings of being overburdened, overworked, overloaded, and overwhelmed. As our energy reservoirs diminish, we may feel drained, weary, worn out, irritable, restless, and on edge. Fatigue—exhaustion—may set in. Moreover, as we fret about completing commitments, we may have trouble sleeping, suffer severe headaches or digestive disturbances, and in short find ourselves incapable of enjoying life and experiencing pleasure. When this happens, we frequently become cranky, impatient, and too often easily annoyed about matters of minor consequence.

This ongoing strain on our bodies interferes with our sensations, stifles release, and limits self-expression. These impediments generate the biochemical and physiological components of stress. Being so out of touch with ourselves impedes our very feelings of being ourselves. Our bodies become tense, hard, and tight. Muscles contract and constrict, reducing blood circulation. And blood, as we all know, is the lifeline delivering oxygen and nourishment to every cell in our bodies. If we remain stressed, our bodies tend to become stiff and excessively tense, which, in turn, causes premature fatigue, tightening of the muscles, and general inflexibility. As muscles constrict, movement is restricted, even blocked. Excessive tension inhibits breathing and limits oxygen intake, which interferes with physical sensation.

We grow tense whenever we try to do too much in too little time. The chatter inside us increases in volume and noise fills our head. We often experience this noise as the barking of orders or the nagging whine of critical judgments directed toward ourselves or others. The complexity involved in the way we have internalized our need to control and be on top of all situations is what most often prevents us from turning down the noise and subduing the insanity.

Efforts to control always lead to tension. In its wake, the intensity with which we strive to get things done, accomplish tasks, and achieve results creates stress in our bodies. As tension increases, our consciousness becomes dulled, our awareness decreases, and our attentiveness dissipates. With increased fatigue, our efficiency and performance skills decline. We frequently react by increasing our efforts, which, of course, creates more tension and leads to almost inevitable failure.

Fatigue can also work to protect us as it may make us aware of our great need to rest. Indeed, excessive muscle tension can literally hold us down. The persistence of contracted muscles exacts a lot of energy, and the numbing fatigue that ensues limits our endurance. This decrease in energy and this sapping of our vitality signal that our fires are dying out. At these moments, we can become overwhelmed by our work and the excessive tension brought on by its demands.

We hope that one day we will become wise to our treadmill existence and listen to our bodies crying out for rest. Most people recognize that such moments warrant a short break, a pause in search of rest. Herein lies the process by which we deliberately structure our time for rest.

Arriving at Rest

We often equate rest solely with physical repose. The concept, however, is much broader and encompasses physical, mental, and spiritual dimensions. In turn, rest in all its dimensions grants us the power to go on.

Breathing affects our ability to rest. We can stop and experience the sensation of breath itself. We follow our breathing, relax into it, and thus begin to experience ourselves. All this brings us more into our bodies. Getting down to feeling ourselves breathe in and then letting go of the breath allows us to become more in touch with our bodies. The more effortless our breathing is, the gentler, slower, and deeper it becomes. Thus, being in touch with our bodies frees our minds from distracting thoughts and we become calmer. By remaining grounded in the overall sensation of being in our bodies in a nonjudgmental, neutrally detached manner, we permit ourselves deep relaxation, opening up to what is in and all around us. Such bodily relaxation helps us to live in our bodies in a more vital, gentle, effortless, and serene way. The result is that our bodies take on an ease of movement, a marked increase in gracefulness, poise, and fluidity.

As we relax and sense our bodies as a whole, we experience ourselves moving through life from a deep place of physical ease, inner strength, and profound serenity. Physical ease is reflected in mental clarity and emotional detachment. Slowly, we begin to make being comfortable in our bodies more important than getting things done. We begin to feel free of tension and become much more alert. Soon our bodies come to a standstill and are transformed into a site for rest.

What does it mean to arrive at rest in our bodies? We begin to rest when we let go of constant efforts and struggles to make our lives happen. From the onset, we must seek ways to let go of tension, loosen the tightness, and dispel the relentless pursuit of doing.

Furthermore, to rest one's body means to trust enough to surrender by letting go. How? Resting allows us to release stress and avoid fatigue and thereby be at ease. As we rest in our bodies, we begin to move more slowly, gently, and effortlessly. As our bodies relax, we feel ourselves quieting down to the point where we enter a calm and calming space. In that space, we free ourselves from the weight of thought and expectations. As we slow down, we become more focused and better able to concentrate at a deeper level.

This ability to focus and concentrate engages us so completely that we experience an emptying of the mind, which allows us a deeper sense of our bodies' calm, stillness, peace, and inner quiet. In such a space, we are able to listen to ourselves and our environment. By resting in our bodies, we restore a sense of dignity while realizing that ordinary life is enough in itself. This is to say, we come to appreciate how by resting in the simple and the ordinary, we come to be at home with ourselves.

We feel a profound sense of serenity, ease, comfort, and peace. An inner relaxation permeates our rest. We often find ourselves softening our touch, easing our grip, walking with a lighter gait, and even opening doors with less and less force. These and other manifestations tell us that we are reaping the benefits of that proper rest we all so earnestly seek and so very much require.

When we rest, we occupy space naturally and measure time in a very particular manner. And each of us appears to inhabit space and mark time somewhat differently. That is, we all exhibit a certain style or distinctive know-how in this regard.

Where Do We Find Rest?

Where is it that we find rest? One illustrative, useful image that comes to mind is of a water lily serenely floating at rest on the surface of a pond. This image serves to remind us that resting emerges, occurs, happens in a particular space or better, a defined place, a specific environment. In this environment, I cease to act, do, work and thus stop physical and emotional effort. I free myself from worry, anxiety, and a sense of vulnerability because in this space, this environment, I can pause, settle down, and experience a sense of arrival. As I surrender to this place, I find myself as though landing, letting go, and allowing myself to be supported by this place's very foundations.

Spaces, then, are pauses that can ground us for a brief moment, an hour, a day, or longer. These pauses constitute and define our style of rest. Our typical response is to feel safe, secure, supported, and belonging in that space. Moreover, we feel welcomed and at home. In addition, the space elicits a readiness to yield outwardly to the support bearing our weight beneath us, as it were. As a result, we feel free enough to let ourselves be held and embraced by the space. We also experience a release from our addiction to continual striving when we give ourselves over to the place of rest. Letting go thus becomes our highest priority and it is here, in this space, that we find a place in which to dwell, to abide.

More and more, as we yield to the support of our space and surrender to our environment, we come to greater rest. And any space can become a resting place. We may find rest upon a mat, a bed, in a chair, on a couch, on the grass or ground, on a beach, or in the water. We rest on or upon a thing, in a place, or through some person. By this process, our bodies effortlessly, confidently, and with trust allow themselves to be supported by their entire environment of people, events, and things. The invitation to surrender deeper and deeper into the space offers an opportunity for our bodies, our minds, and our spirits to sink into rest. There, we bring ourselves into peaceful harmony with the world around us.

Surrender to the Now

Rest is also facilitated by a particular time, a particular style of using time. The next great question then is: When does one rest?

We begin to rest at that moment when we stop getting ready to do this and that. We will find rest primarily when we surrender to the now, the present moment, the present reality. In rest, we abandon ourselves, we give ourselves over to the present moment.

Moreover, in moving from doing to being, we stop and pause. When living in the awareness of the present moment, it is as if we were being massaged by a certain kind of time. When we are no longer on the move, when we are no longer hurrying, racing, pushing in a battle in the strenuous struggle against time, we start to let go of this stance toward time and assume a more relaxed flow with the present moment. We no longer become possessed by the past or the future, and time slowly disappears as we give ourselves over to the present moment. In the present moment, we become at ease with time, serene with time, and at peace with time.

Supported by a space in which we feel at home and by a sense of time in the present moment, we are able to rest. As we allow ourselves to be supported by our environment of people, events, and things, we are able to enhance our ability to rest in our bodies as well as in the sanctuaries of our inner selves. As we grow more and more capable of being ourselves, we respond with ever greater ease by resting in our internal experience of peace with ourselves and others.

From this inclination toward rest, we come to dwell in the now as we submerge into our innermost selves. We become self-possessed and we take up our everyday lives in a more effortless manner while we lightly hold time and space about us.

Authentic rest is marked by an effortlessness, a non-doing. This involves moving deeper and deeper into a gut feeling of physical ease. Here in the present moment and in an at-home space, as we stop trying, we simply let be. Likewise, we focus on our internal process and not on our external goals and results.

But in order to rest we need to remain fully and consciously aware, ever able to notice, recognize, and attend to our style of living. We must be able to pay attention to how we are doing and what we are doing. We must, likewise, pay attention to our environment, that is, how we maintain sensitive contact with our environment. By practicing detachment, we will be able to grow in inner strength, experience more profound internal peace and enjoy a calm vitality. Our physical ease will flow, and our energy will continue to sustain us as we conduct our lives in a more restful manner. From a perspective focusing upon rest, we find ourselves in an ever-better position to allow people, events, and things to be as they are.

Rest is critical in making possible the unfolding human experience of hospitality. Rest helps us become centered, grounded, and connected to ourselves, others, and God. Living from a position of spiritually formative rest allows us to pray ceaselessly. In this way, we are always at prayer.

Anchoring our everyday living in rest, even as rest provides the grounding to be and to do, enables us to welcome people into our lives. What results is the capacity to make room in our lives for ourselves, for others, and for God. We recognize rest as a foundational dimension of our lives. In addition, we see in rest a way of keeping it simple in life and a path to tranquility. What rest provides to our ordinary lives is an ability to nurture a sense of ease, gratitude, and peace.

– 7 –

Being Yourself

As we come to the last phase of our descriptive definition of hospitality — be yourself, I turn to the Italian language for some assistance. Be yourself, in Italian, is *sii te stesso*. The literal translation is simply "Be yourself."

What is this invitation to be yourself? In a world that emphasizes measuring up, conforming to what society wants you to be, the simple advice to be yourself is taken for granted and does not register consciously.

Someone affirming the need for me to be myself in a situation is not the usual way people engage with me. The usual underlying message is: You need to be who you are supposed to be.

Growing up, there was always the instruction, the message of the Greek chorus saying: You should, must, have to be, this or that. Recently, the therapeutic culture has generated an enormous bill for the transformation, the movement, from feeling controlled by the should, must, have to positions to one of being free to be yourself. Insurance companies and private pay clients have spent millions of dollars on this readjustment process.

Fundamental Dimensions Shape Our Lives

Even if you are relatively inwardly free to respond to the exclamation to Be yourself!, the question still stands: what does it mean for you to be yourself? As we previously explored, we all have been formed and shaped by various historical human dimensions. We all have had three fundamental dimensions that shaped our everyday lives: the vital, the functional, and the spirit dimensions.

My situation of sitting at my desk and writing this chapter about being myself is a good example. On the vital level of this experience, I am able to sit at my desk with energy, focus, and concentration. This is supported by a good night's sleep, a healthy breakfast, and some exercise. I feel supported by my body to think, to coordinate my movements to write, and to sit in my seventy-five-year-old swivel chair. My physical/bodily dimension is relaxed, healthy, and peaceful.

On the functional/executive dimension of being at my desk, I am organized, have a plan, and know how to apply my skills to write this book. I find myself disciplined, systematic, and focused on completing my task of writing for three hours in the early morning every day.

The spiritual dimension of this morning's writing situation is anchored in a prayerful presence of leisurely allowing my creativity to flow from the mystery of my life, my life experience. In my stance of willing, allowing, and connecting with my inner self, my inner spirit, I find myself inspired by my attitude of openness, surrender, and letting be. As I sit here pausing and pondering, cautioning myself not to try too hard or bear down on making it happen, I pull myself back, breathe, look around the room, listen to the sounds of the birds, and wait.

This moment of waiting is supported by trust and confidence in the creative process. It is a struggle, a back and forth of believing, trusting, having faith, and then, fear, anxiety, concern that the well may be dry.

Being Yourself

The gift of the thought is that I am not alone in this moment. The presence of the mystery is holding me. In my breathing, I trust that I remember that it is not all up to me. I am only a part of a process. I need to trust and relax in the presence of the mystery. Rest is my mantra. I let go, just be, and keep my hands open.

I feel energized pausing, remembering, and settling down. Reconnected to the project at hand, I find myself moving forward, just allowing the words to flow.

Being myself is grounded in the vital, functional, and spirit dimensions of my life. Paying attention to my vital dimension helps me to be more vibrantly alive. I find myself growing in confidence and competence in my functional ability to keep on writing and making sense of the phrase being myself. Ultimately, I continue to practice resting in the presence of the mystery in my life and trust that the mystery is inspiring me, breathing into me an openness to receive what comes forth from the stillness.

The process of hospitality extends a particular invitation: Welcome and make yourself at home, so you may rest and be yourself. In hospitality, you are offered space and time, a safe harbor, a secure place, a sanctuary, a home where you can find peace.

As you look to your everyday experience, you discover that you tend to take the experience of being yourself for granted. What is being yourself all about? What are the dimensions, qualities, and descriptors of being yourself?

In everyday life, people struggle to be themselves. We hear people saying that they went to a certain event and felt they could not be themselves. When we are with certain people, we believe we just can't be ourselves. At work, many people simply find themselves unable to be themselves. Others say that they cannot let their hair down, they need to be a certain way, need to be just so, that they are tense, pulled back, or simply can't relax.

Where do you find yourself able to be yourself? Many respond that occurs in situations where they feel safe, secure, comfortable, relaxed, and at home.

In everyday life experience, being yourself means that you are able to be true, real, authentic, genuine, and sincere. Whether it is a moment, a situation, an experience, a manner, or style, being yourself is being original, unique, congenial, and confident with who you are. It has to do with depth, interiority, inwardness, self-possession, consciousness, and awareness. Being yourself means that you are consistent, coherent, and in harmony with your real self. In being yourself, you are faithful, constant, persistent, willing, effective, and thus loyal to who you are. Being natural, at ease, content, spontaneous, simple, and familiar are also parts of being yourself. You have a relaxed presence to reality.

To be yourself means that you allow yourself to unfold that inner something that frees you to come to life as a unique person. In this state, you are comfortable letting down, surrendering, and allowing your complete individuality to emerge easily and spontaneously. Here you are able to sing your song and dance your dance.

From this stance of being yourself, you do not have to be cautious or careful about who you are. Rather, you have the capacity to make choices. In being conscious and explicit in your choice making, you become the originator, the crafter of your motives and innovations. This means that you pay attention to the common ways of living as you try to be in accordance with your actual self, conforming to reality.

When you are living from your essential, true self, you are in possession of yourself. You feel confident, self-reliant, and focused on taking up your reality in an open, single-minded, dedicated manner that is deliberate and intentional. The more you can patiently listen to, attend to, be present to, stay with, put a name to what you experience, the more you can be yourself and like yourself.

In being self-possessed, you can stand alone, be upright, not self-conscious, and maintain a healthy detachment that allows your life to flow. You are willing and trusting enough to just let things happen. Being self-possessed allows more self-respect to unfold. You grow in appreciation of your true self, your inner self. In respect, you bring to light the splendor of values hidden in yourself, in others, and in your surroundings. You are able to value yourself.

Being valued calls you to be yourself. In the process of being yourself, you continue to create and build a home in the world and feel at home in it. Having a stable and well-functioning ego, you are rooted, centered in your home, and this enables you to live out your experience in a personal, unique, and original way.

From this perspective of being respectful toward yourself, you can detect the truth, beauty, and goodness of who you are. This is rooted in the spontaneous appreciation of your worth. Looking again, looking twice at yourself and others, paying benevolent attention to and casting the good upon yourself and others makes you more sensitive to any value in others and yourself.

Self-respect cultivates personal dignity, a sense of natural pride in yourself. Being in harmony with yourself, feeling self-confident and competent, and having your feet planted on the ground helps you feel connected to your body's reality. Living in your body with dignity, you carry yourself, move, and hold your body in such a manner that you feel that your being is good enough. Your bearing indicates that you know your feelings in such a sensitive manner as to inspire and command respect. As your body is straight with your head held high, you go slow, are stately, and have time to be and to feel. This dignified stance makes you fundamentally worthy of respect.

Other characteristics of being yourself and having a sense of self emerge from a historical background of being loved, accepted, and approved. This affirmation enables you to be centered, grounded, and rooted such that you feel solid, secure, tranquil, balanced, connected, and anchored in your own depth and interiority. Comfortable with being who you are, you are able to surrender, have faith in, let go, and be open to simply being and living fully consciously in the present moment.

The host invites the guest to be themselves. How does it come about that the guest feels comfortable enough to let down, let go, surrender, and be themselves? This process of the guest being themselves is facilitated by the host. It is extended by the host to the guest.

The host is already at home and, to whatever extent possible, is being himself. It is the guest who is the outsider in this place to which they have been invited. The question becomes: What does it mean to the guest to respond to the invitation from the host to make themselves at home and be themselves?

Discovering the I Am

In hospitality, you are offered space and time, a safe harbor, a secure place, a sanctuary, a home where you can find peace and at-homeness. The space offered to the guest by the host is their home. They have made this space where the guest can be themselves. The host wants to share their space with the guest and hopes that the guest can find the environment to be a place where they also can find peace and be themselves.

The guest feels, senses, and understands that the host means what they say. There is a presence about the host that conveys to the guest that they are honest, authentic, and genuine in this invitation to be themselves in his home.

The guest intuits that the host is a person of their word. They are a person who loves their neighbor as themselves. Maybe this is the key that allows the guest to take their proper place in the home of the host. How has the host come to a place in their life that they can invite the outsider, the guest, to be themselves as the host is in this home?

The host invites the guest just to be. They invite the guest to rest. They make it clear that the guest does not have to *do* anything.

The host has learned from experience that in just being, they come home to themselves. They light up within themselves. They come to life. They feel alive. They emerge and unfold.

Letting go, letting down, surrendering, the host has discovered the power in just being. They uncover their *I am.* In this *I am,* the host realizes they can be their most human self. This reminds me of Popeye the Sailor. A fictional, muscular, cartoon character, Popeye seems bereft of manners and uneducated. He does not pretend or play roles. In proclaiming, "I yam what I yam and dat's all what I yam," the cartoon character speaks about being himself. It is a powerful piece of lived wisdom. Popeye cannot be anyone other than who he is.

Perhaps that is what the host came to discover in their process of becoming themselves as a human being. But what were the facilitating conditions for them to grow into being themselves? The act of self-acceptance comes to mind.

Self-acceptance is a process of willingly receiving, admitting, and making peace with who you are. This means that you make the effort to know yourself as you are. This happens by being open, paying attention to how you find yourself being who you are with yourself and others. As you slow down and see and hear how you are engaged with yourself, with people, events, and things in your everyday life experience, you will uncover your style of being you.

Naming, claiming, and seeing your style of being yourself without judgment allows you to blow up, make more explicit what is implicit in your style of being who you are.

Accepting who and what I am is a process of taking myself up with respect and reverence. It is looking at myself with appreciative attention and thoughtful care and concern. In connecting with my actual self, I am able to affirm and confirm that who and what I am is good. Self-acceptance is taking myself up as having value, worth, and importance. It is a process of acquiring the wisdom to take care of myself.

Self-acceptance is loving oneself. It is being patient, kind, and gentle. It is holding myself lightly, respectfully, and reverently.

Self-acceptance is being a witness, an observer, a watchful presence. It is accepting what is, saying yes to the present moment. With sustained constant attention you simply watch the now of the moment. You are at ease. You are not the doer, but just being, just being at ease.

In this moment, in this situation, in this style of self-acceptance, your mind is not racing, planning, functioning at full throttle, but feeling vulnerable and insecure. A sense of lacking or incompleteness, of not being whole, seems to be driving your life and preventing you from being in the now. As long as you are stuck in your past identity or the feeling that only the future holds promise of salvation or fulfillment, you cannot slow down and connect with yourself.

In this wave of pushing and compulsively striving, you can get lost in the hecticness of your everyday life, lost in any sense of being awake, aware, and alert. Actually, the result of all this ego devotion of effort and energy leads to at least a low level of discontent or nervousness and ultimately sleeping the great sleep of non-presence to yourself and the world around you.

Self-acceptance is not a self-approval, but a seeing of self without judgment. In self-acceptance, I discover my own inner strength. I clearly see my shortcomings, too. My sense of self is derived from a deeper and truer place within myself.

In the experience of being myself, I enter the present of the moment. I discover that the present is all there is. It all happens in the now. I honor and give full attention to the now of the moment. My attention is truly in the now. My attention is essential. It is being conscious of my present.

To stay present in everyday life, it helps to be deeply rooted within yourself, to be absolutely awake, and still.

We are called to live in the mystery. As you listen with your third ear, you hear in the stillness the call from the mystery to take up your gift and be yourself. As you give up your egoic self that you have created on your own, there seems to be more room to hear the voice of your deepest self, whom the mystery calls you to be.

This path of being yourself, invites you to find your true self, your most authentic self, in your daily life. In the mundane activities of daily living, you are called to live in the mystery. You are called to be willing to listen. What matters is listening to the still small voice in the here and now that calls you to be yourself. As you continue to grow into being your authentic and genuine self, you hold yourself lightly, gently, and graciously.

The experience of being yourself is a process of being deeply and fully connected with your body in its vital dimension. It is an ongoing process of forming and shaping a stable and well-functioning ability to manage, control, make, design, plan, execute, achieve, and carry out your daily activities in an effortless and humble manner. Being yourself is living your life from your spiritual dimension, a place where you simply allow yourself to be who you are. Compassionately and tenderly, you hold yourself in the palms of your hands with awe, wonder, mystery, appreciation, acceptance, and gratitude.

Being yourself is a gift from all the people who have cultivated you along the way, who have cared for you since the moment of your conception. The mystery of the unfolding of being able to be yourself calls forth in you a strong stirring that raises your mind and heart to the mystery, proclaiming that it is all good. The mystery continues to call you to simply be yourself through the people, events, and things of your daily living.

The guest has respect for their host. They are willing to be influenced by the host. They are open to encountering their host. The welcomer makes themself available to their guest. This allows the host and guest to be in touch with each other. The guest makes themselves receptive to the host and gives themselves freely to the host. The welcomer gives to the guest the opportunity to speak to them as a host who is willing to be spoken to.

The host has evolved over time in their ability to be gentle, tender, and fragile. Able to be themselves, the host has developed a type of human presence that realizes the dimension of discretion. This particular style of human presence makes the home a place of welcome, of hospitality, a field of intimacy.

The welcomer invites the guest to be themselves, to make themselves at home in the welcomer's space. Over time, the welcomer has become an informed citizen in the common ways of life.

The welcomer is a practitioner of discretion. They have become a wise person, a person of unusual learning, judgment, and insight. All of this wisdom has emerged from their learned understanding and respect for the common ways of life.

One of those common ways that has been passed on over the centuries is loving your neighbor as yourself. Most religious traditions have some form of this insight as part of their everyday practice of life. It has been integrated into the common ways, the common manner of being with other human beings.

Thinking what is best, what is good, what is the common good, is grounded in the dynamics of loving your neighbor as yourself. It has grown out of a tradition of being civilized, of growing deeper and deeper in answering the call of being human.

Love of one's neighbor is a general and regular attitude that guides the conduct of the welcomer to the guest. Love of the neighbor as oneself fulfills the law of the Old and the New Testaments. The welcomer, a welcomer to the guest, is grounded in love, and their love is their guide of conduct. It is the love that the welcomer extends to the guest that brings the guest to life.

As the welcomer matures in their humanness, their love for the guest becomes more selfless. They grow in their ability to overcome their egoic reaction of fear, insecurity, arrogance, and pride in relationship to the guest. As the welcomer grows in self-acceptance and love of neighbor as themselves, they become more in touch with their limitedness, their finitude, their egoic residue, their weakness.

As the welcomer ripens their ability to be tactful, discrete, and prudent in their ways of being human, the guest feels a warmer, more natural reception from the host. It is in this warmth, patience, kindness, appreciation by the welcomer the guest is able to let down, let go, and surrender their egoic, reactive mode. They no longer resist the love of neighbor that the welcomer offers to them.

The host has a history of gradually growing into the ability to welcome the guest. Over time, the host has become able to feel comfortable in themselves. With this strength in themselves, they are able to reach out and just be with their guest. In this stance of just being, the guest is empowered by the presence of the host to rest and be themselves.

The guest's response to their host's presence is to slowly let down, let go, and surrender. Their figurative breast plate, armor, defensive wall, crumble. They begin to feel safe, secure, and at home. Their body intuits that this space is comfortable, and they are able to graciously respond to the host's invitation. The host is perceived by the guest as authentic, as real, as actual. The aura around the host is a sense of being fully trustworthy and genuine. This sense of presence of the host, the ability of the host to be themselves, calls forth the guest also to be their true self.

The guest experiences the host as embodying the second of the two great commandments: Love your neighbor as yourself.

The guest senses that the host loves themselves. The host knows that they can only begin to become themselves when they accept who and what they are.

When I look into the face of the other, when I look into the eyes of the other, I see and experience a call to responsibility. I am awake and become aware that the face, the eyes that I encounter is my neighbor. More than 2,000 years of wisdom well up inside of me. I am to love my neighbor as myself. This counsel, admonition, formative directive establishes the other who is opposite me as my neighbor. There are no ifs, ands, or buts that this human being is my neighbor. It is my moral imperative to encounter this other as my neighbor.

Connected to my moral consciousness, I see and hear with my heart that the stranger, the other is not just my guest. They are my neighbor whom I am commanded to love as myself.

What I am describing is that in inviting the guest to be themselves, the host is coming from a perspective of invitation. The welcomer invites the guest to be present, to participate in the experience of being at home in this space. But at the same time, the welcomer is called to remember that they are also rooted in a tradition that recognizes the other as neighbor.

This remembrance is not just a statement, a report of a fact, or an opinion. It is hoped the welcomer has integrated this venerable ancient commandment into their consciousness, so that it is not just another bit of information that is carried around in their head.

The welcomer over time has matured in understanding the "love of neighbor as myself" as a guiding principle that has become part of their consciousness. It is part of the way they see and hear. It has become part of their way of being whole-hearted in their presence to the stranger, the guest, the neighbor.

Having been received by others, I am able to be myself. I can only begin to become myself when I accept who and what I am. I am a human being. Being myself means that I am authentic. I am real. I am actual. I am existing in reality as I am. There is nothing false, fake, or counterfeit about me. I am not in the practice of deceiving by pretending that I am someone different from who I really am. I am not trying to be anything that I am not. To be genuine and consistent with who I am is what I am trying to be about in my everyday life.

Being myself means to be authentic. I am trying to live my life aligned in accordance with the real and actual truths and facts of my story, my narrative, my history.

As a human being, I am committed to acquiring wisdom to take good care of myself. By taking good care of myself, I am better able to take care of my neighbor. The host helps the guest to be themselves by cultivating their presence as a host. It is an embodiment of the second great commandment, love your neighbor as yourself.

When I am the most free to be myself, I am able to be the most fully present to the stranger, the guest, my neighbor. As I accept my limits, and just be authentically who I am, I am embracing my finitude and my imperfections. With courage and persistence, I am able to see and accept my egoic needs to be special and self-centered.

With humility, I admit that I am powerless over being totally in control of my reality. At any moment, my profound vulnerability may be disclosed to me. The Coronavirus is staring me right in the face as I write this. A doctor could disclose that I may have only a few months to live. A sudden fall down the stairs could be the end of me.

If I focused on how powerless I really am in light of all that is, I could feel that my life is unmanageable. At any moment, I could experience myself in a state of quiet egoic desperation.

At any time in our lives, we could be taking our last breath. I say all of this not to scare you or myself, but simply to admit the truth. Any moment could be our last. At any moment, that moment could be my last. By speaking this truth, meditating on it, I can embrace it as my truth and fundamental reality.

As I grow in maturity, through my self-awareness and self-knowledge, I can see more clearly who and what I really am. I appreciate more wholeheartedly my creatureliness. In humility, I remember who I am and that I can at any moment find myself powerless and my life unmanageable.

Having eyes to see, ears to hear, and a heart to feel, I become awake, aware, and alive to how dependent I am upon others to be kind, caring, and concerned about my well-being. I am dependent upon others to keep me alive.

We are all interconnected. People in the fields are planting and harvesting the food for my table. The medical rescue squad is on standby, ready to render service to me if I need them.

The Coronavirus continues to remind us how powerless and unmanageable our lives can really be. Our interconnectedness with others can provide us solace, a sense of relief, and consolation that we are not alone. In being open and receptive to loving my neighbor as myself, I am practicing the truth that has been disclosed to us for more than 2,000 years.

I am ready, willing, and able to love my neighbor as myself. This means I am committed to care for, attend to, and assume responsibility to love my neighbor as myself.

… 8 …

Conclusion

What does it mean to be human? For more than fifty years, this has been a foundational and fundamental question of my life. It has been a formative question that has guided me into researching the qualities of hospitality. This book is the result of a systematic, rigorous, and disciplined approach to understanding the everyday life experience of hospitality.

The metaphoric image of a stethoscope helps us understand the process used in this book to articulate the essence, the structure of the human experience of hospitality. The stethoscope, a tool of healthcare professionals, is an acoustic medical instrument for listening to internal sounds of the human body such as in the heart, lungs, or abdomen.

In our pursuit to make our implicit understanding of hospitality explicit, the invisible more visible, we have come to use our metaphorical stethoscope to listen to the everyday life sounds of hospitality. I started this listening process by describing my various childhood experiences of receiving hospitality.

My Aunt Sunny and her husband, Wilfred, Nonna, Mémé and Pépé, became characters in my story of receiving hospitality. I felt the same welcome walking onto the land of Julie Country Day School almost every day as a grammar school student. This embrace by the land was buried deep within my body. My memory brings back the warmth, the peace, the sacredness I experienced strolling through its English-style landscape. Its flora and fauna soothed me and brought about a restful mode of consciousness. My body was able to feel the silence and stillness of the land of Julie Country Day. This daily experience of hospitality, where I felt invited and welcomed into my home away from home, gave me a sense of welcome. Julie Country Day School was a marker event of my childhood where I found peace and was able to be myself.

Given the detailed descriptions of hospitality at Mémé and Pépé's, Nonna's, and Julie Country Day, I proceeded to reflect upon and make sense of what these characters and events were disclosing about the phenomenon of hospitality. I came to articulate hospitality as a human experience that is a process which welcomes, invites another to make themselves at home in the welcomer's space to rest and be themselves. Welcome, make yourself at home in order to rest and be yourself has been a guiding principle in my life. I described how that came to be and what it meant in writing this book.

In my quest to come to grips with my perennial question—what does it mean to be human?—I found myself taking up the project of understanding the human qualities of hospitality as providing assistance in answering this perpetual, persistent, re-searching question. I had the intuition that the understanding hospitality would help me understand what it means to be human.

The human experience of hospitality has been evolving since the beginning of human existence. We were welcomed by the planet Earth and invited to make ourselves at home on it. Hospitality became a stance, a posture, a way of life, a way of being. It was a custom, a tradition in which a human being, or a group of human beings, offered, invited, an outsider, a stranger, a foreigner, into their space, their home.

This means that from the beginning there was a host and a guest. The host invites, welcomes, receives, and becomes open to the other.

From this perspective, the host can be the planet Earth, the sky, the heavens, mortals, and or the gods. One could speak of the hospitality of the cosmos, nature, the interpersonal, the personal, and the transcendent. There is also commercial, functional, and entertaining hospitality.

The Old and New Testaments speak of hospitality. All spiritual paths address the theme of hospitality. The Hospitallers in the twelfth century offered food and lodging to pilgrims in the Crusade.

The stranger's need for food and shelter led to the development of the hospitality and tourism industries. The hospitality industry later commodified hospitality and commercialized it. Hospitality has been associated with food, leisure travel and tourism, lodging and recreation. In the industry, the word hospitality is closely linked to the business of hospitality.

Hospitality represents an important dimension of what it means to be human. It is a virtue, a mode of consciousness, that emphasizes that the stranger becomes our sibling. The host welcomes the guest and invites their guest to make themselves at home, to rest and be themselves.

We saw the movie, *Blow-Up*, as an example of a photographic process of making explicit what is implicit. Blowing up the metaphorical pixels of hospitality disclosed its essence, its structure.

Understanding the dimensions of hospitality can assist us in growing deeper and becoming more hospitable to the Earth, to ourselves, and to others. Mother Earth has welcomed us and has offered us her bounty. We, in turn, need to become more hospitable to the Earth and graciously receive her gift as sacred.

By magnifying the pixels of hospitality, we have created, we made the invisible visible, and the implicit explicit. My hope is that I have presented the case that hospitality, as a mode of consciousness, can become a transformative dimension in our egoically oriented culture. Through this perspective on hospitality, I propose moving the culture, and the individuals who comprise it, forward. The move is from a stance of greed and self-interest to one of being graciously welcoming of the guest. Rather than acting hospitably toward the guest or stranger for our own profit, we selflessly invite the guest and welcome them into our space. In so doing, we hope they can find a peaceful place where they can be at home, rest, and be themselves. The hope is that the guest can and will pass that peace on to others.

As I reflect on my experience of hospitality, I received eye contact, a smile, a hug, and some food. I was treated as a sacred guest who was attended to with care, concern, and generosity. I was helped to grow into loving my neighbor as myself, which seems to me to be a critically important part of what it means to be human and cultivate a healthy soul.

Hospitality is an honorable, noble virtue that cultivates moral goodness. It fosters receptivity, openness, graciousness, generosity, and openheartedness. It is a mode of consciousness that can contribute to the common good.

The experience of hospitality continues an historical tradition passed on by our ancestors. Our predecessors embraced the heritage of this moral value common to all human beings. This common value of welcoming the stranger, the other, can now assist us in combatting environmental degradation and in supporting displaced people whatever the cause of their displacement.

However, within our culture that emphasizes individualism and functionalism, achievement and success, greed, self-interest and profit, a significant displacement of values has occurred. Hospitality has been displaced as a disposition, a consciousness that helps individuals and a more humane attitude toward all life around us.

The process of the displacement of hospitality as a common way of being has a deeper origin of being covered over as we live our everyday lives. Striving for success, affirmation, and security through prosperity has displaced the value of the sacred in everyday living.

The struggle with the COVID-19 pandemic has pulled back the taken-for-granted curtain around our ability to breathe on our own. A moment of struggling with our breathing immediately alerts us to how significant this gift is in our lives. Television images of the breathing tubes in people who have been intubated to bring oxygen to their lungs shake our confidence that we will always be able to rely on our ability to breathe on our own.

Breathing is an everyday function we take for granted until the moment we struggle to breathe. From the very beginning of the Genesis story of creation in the Old Testament, we are introduced to Yahweh breathing life into Adam and Eve. We celebrate newborns naturally taking their first breaths.

The sacred in the everyday has been displaced by various egoic values and replaced with functional values that cultivate an overemphasis on functionalism. Functionalism combined with individualism ramps up the egoic attitude of striving to be on top and in control of everything.

From this narrative, the portrait of the sacred is covered over, concealed, and lost in the everyday hectic activities of the musts and shoulds that make up a style of human living all too common in our culture today.

I am not encouraging you to become hypervigilant, analytical, introspective, or overly focused on putting yourself under a microscope. I am recommending tuning into a sense of how you find yourself in the moment. This is a moment of coming home to yourself and hearing with your inner ears, seeing with your inner eyes, and listening to your inner heart. In this pause it is important to ask: How am I present to myself as a human being who is growing into hospitality? Am I gracious toward myself? Are my movements smooth, easeful, slow, and graceful? Is my speech clear, direct, inviting, and connecting? Is my breathing full, free, and lively? Is my breathing facilitating my life force, my breath of life, to animate and radiate a peaceful presence as a person of hospitality?

The culture continues to trend toward the morass of narcissism. This focusing and living from the egoic of our personhood is a major obstacle to the unfolding of hospitality in our culture.

Deeply disturbing are the images of police and the military dressed top to bottom in protective gear trying to combat a mob intent on halting the peaceful transfer of power in the United States Capitol or in response to widespread protests against police brutality and systemic racism incited by the police murder of George Floyd, an unarmed Black man. In this battle, there is the covering over and forgetting that we are called to be human and to stand out in the world as a welcomer, a host to that neighbor, and to love that neighbor as ourselves.

The disposition of hospitality can become a way, an approach to the other, that can bring peace to ourselves, others, and the world.

From the perspective of hospitality, I have the responsibility and obligation to the other, to my neighbor, to build a fire and invite the other to warm themselves, let down, let go, surrender, and enter into this inviting space where they may feel welcomed to rest and be themselves.

This book illuminates a new perspective through which to understand hospitality. This perspective emerges through an existential-phenomenological research approach. This simply means that the richness of this inquiry emphasizes grounding the phenomenon of hospitality in the very essence of what it is to be human.

We have tried to understand the what, the quiddity of hospitality as it discloses itself in everyday life experience. This has necessitated the development of a language to articulate what is the human experience of hospitality.

My focus has been on the disposition of hospitality. The culture has covered over the disposition by reducing it to a function. Hospitality, as a disposition, is a way of life, not just a moment of entertaining guests.

As a personal disposition, the welcomer, the host, continues to strive to deepen their ability to help the guest to feel invited and welcomed, to be able to make themselves at home in order to rest and be themselves.

Devotion to hospitality in all its dimensions can assist us in becoming better cultural change agents by growing deeper into the practice of being a hospitable practitioner and a more humane human being.

Acknowledgments

Writing a book about hospitality would not be possible without a village. From as far back as I can remember, my village has been welcoming and affirming.

How grateful I am to acknowledge the people in my village who embraced the opportunity to help me explore true hospitality in this book.

I am thankful for the assistance of James Francis P. Stone, a dear friend and valued colleague who holds a master's degree in Psychology, who worked with me daily for two years as I wrote this book. Karen Maguire, my sister-in-law, shared her skills as a professional writer and editor to help transform the manuscript into the book you are reading. Her insightful questions truly helped me clarify and then express all that I wanted to say about what I believe to be the true nature of hospitality.

Several people kindly agreed to read this book while I was writing it. I am especially appreciative of the many who provided specific and helpful feedback, including my sister-in-law Mary Ellen Bilotta, who spent many hours reviewing each chapter with me. My brothers George Bilotta and Mark Bilotta were trusted consultants and advisors throughout this project. My sister Mary Ann (Bilotta) Blackman and my friends Anthony Amico, Teresa Rhodes, and Robert Short provided support and insightful comments. Also providing support and some much needed laughter to me throughout this project was my brother-in-law John W. Gearan, a retired sportswriter and lawyer.

My cousin, Victoria Marrama, daughter of my Uncle Wilfred and Aunt Sunny, affirmed my memories and descriptions of the Italian side of our family. My lifelong friend, Wallace "Wally" Sillanpoa, who grew up in this

Italian neighborhood in Leominster, MA, before going on to earn his doctorate in Italian Studies, listened with reflection and humor as I developed this story about hospitality.

The beautiful art that graces the book's cover is the work of Julie Vaughn Gearan, my niece. Her talent as an award-winning artist is clear in her channeling the true spirit of hospitality theme into the moving image of my hands—open and welcoming.

I am especially thankful to my mother, Kathleen "Kitty" (Becrelis) Bilotta, for listening with love and confirming many of my childhood stories.

About the Author

Long before Vincent M. Bilotta ever dreamed of a career as a psychotherapist with a concentration in Existential Phenomenology, he was fascinated by the concept of hospitality. His earliest memories are steeped in the hospitality bestowed upon him by his extended family, from the richness of nature, and through transformative engagement with fellow humans throughout his life as a son, eldest brother to ten siblings, husband, father, friend, mental health psychotherapist, faculty member, consultant, author, and entrepreneur.

With his wife and life partner, Denise Gearan Bilotta, and their daughters, Kathleen and Angeline, he has generously returned the hospitality that shaped him as a young boy by warmly welcoming visitors into their home and gardens. Their guests, who feel seen, heard, and cared for, frequently are treated to a delightful meal and to Vinnie's booming laugh.

Vincent recently retired after thirty-six years as president and founder of Formation Consultation Services, Inc. (FCS). Through FCS, he provided ongoing formation consulting to religious orders in the United States, Europe, Central America, Australia, and the Caribbean Islands. He served as chief initial ongoing formation consultant to Maryknoll missionary priests and brothers from 1987 to 2002. For a decade beginning in 1976, Vincent provided psychotherapy and directed an educational center at an international therapeutic center for Catholic religious/

clergy in Whitinsville, MA and Natick, MA. He previously worked as a psychologist while serving as a Captain in the U.S. Air Force at Wilford Hall Medical Center in San Antonio, TX, and at the Scott Air Force Base Medical Center in Belleville, IL. While attending Duquesne University, he worked as a psychologist at Woodville State and Dixmont State hospitals from 1968 to 1972.

After receiving bachelor's degrees in philosophy and psychology from the College of the Holy Cross in Worcester, MA, Vincent earned his master's and doctoral degrees in clinical psychology at Duquesne University in Pittsburgh, PA. He also holds a master's degree in Religious Studies from Assumption College in Worcester, MA.

Vincent has lectured the greater Worcester, MA area at Anna Maria College, Assumption College, and the University of Massachusetts Medical Center. In addition, he also was a visiting lecturer at Duquesne University in Pittsburgh, PA.